PLANTAT

BEFORE

EMANCIPATION.

BY

R. Q. MALLARD, D. D.,

NEW ORLEANS, LA.

TO THE MEMORY OF
Charles Colcock Jones, D. D.,

WHO, WHETHER HIS WORK AS A MISSIONARY TO THE BLACKS, OR THE WIDER INFLUENCE OF HIS EXAMPLE, AND WRITINGS IN THEIR BEHALF, BE CONSIDERED, IS JUSTLY ENTITLED TO THE NAME OF THE APOSTLE OF THE NEGRO SLAVES; AND OF HIS MANY FELLOW WORKERS IN THE GOSPEL MINISTRY UPON THE SAME FIELD, ONLY LESS CONSPICUOUS, SELF-DENYING AND USEFUL; AND OF THE HOST OF MASTERS AND MISTRESSES, WHOSE KINDNESS TO THE BODIES, AND EFFORTS FOR THE SALVATION OF THE SOULS OF THE SUBJECT RACE PROVIDENTIALLY PL ACED UNDER THEIR RULE AND CARE, WILL BE READ OUT, WITH THEIR NAMES, IN THE DAY WHEN "THE BOOKS SHALL BE OPENED," AND "GOD SHALL BRING EVERY WORK INTO JUDGMENT, WITH EVERY SECRET THING, WHETHER IT BE GOOD OR WHETHER IT BE EVIL,"

THIS BOOK IS REVERENTLY AND LOVINGLY DEDICATED.

A Word to the Reader.

THE chapters to follow were originally given to the public in the form of a series of letters, under the same title, contributed to the columns of *The Southwestern Presbyterian*, the official organ for over twenty years of the Synod of Mississippi, embracing the greater part of the State of the same name, and the whole of Louisiana. They were suggested by an article copied into that journal from *The New York Evangelist*, and written by a lady, a native of South Carolina, married and resident at the North, in defence of Southern Christian slaveholders from the aspersions of a secretary of the Northern Presbyterian Freedmen's Board.

In this graceful and vigorous vindication of her fellow-countrymen, quotation was made from an old faded copy of a printed report, made by Rev. Charles Colcock Jones, to the Liberty County Georgia "Association for the Religious Instruction of the Colored People." Having in the providence of God been brought into intimate relations with this eminent servant of God, and personal acquaintance with his work, I found that by marriage I had come into possession of a bound volume of pamphlets, containing not only the report cited, but the entire series, thirteen in number, as well as all his many writings upon the same subject. This discovery of accessible and ample material for a fuller vindication of the memory of our ancestors, as well as my relations to the writer, as they constituted peculiar qualifications for, so they seemed to constitute a providential call to the work.

These letters, thus prepared, met with general favor among the readers of our journal, and at the suggestion of white and black, and by the advice of prominent ministers of more than one denomination, they are now published in book form and seek a larger audience.

The purpose of the author has been to portray a civilization now obsolete, to picture the relations of mutual attachment and kindness which in the main bound together master and servant, and to give this and future generations some correct idea of the noble work done by Southern masters and mistresses of all denominations for the salvation of the slave.

If the reader shall have half the pleasure in perusing that the author has had in writing these letters; if they shall in any degree contribute to the restoration of the mutual relations of kindness and confidence characterizing the old regimé, and sorely strained, not so much by emancipation, as by the unhappy happy events immediately succeeding it; if through the blessing of him "who hath made of one blood all nations of men," North and South, shall be induced to join hands and hearts in generous, confiding and harmonious co-operative work for the salvation and consequent elevation of this race, dwelling with us in our common heritage, then will the author's purpose have been fully realized, and the country will have made sensible progress toward the solution of the race question, and the church gratifying advance in the settlement of a more interesting and important problem: How shall Africa in America be won for Christ?

R. Q. MALLARD.

NEW ORLEANS, LOUISIANA, *December*, 1891.

PLANTATION LIFE BEFORE EMANCIPATION.

CHAPTER I.

REASONS FOR WRITING AND TOPICS OF LETTERS.

IT was in May, 1864, that Johnson issued his celebrated battle-order at Cass Station, on the line of the Atlantic and Western railroad. Our forces were in fine trim, anxious for the fray, and confident of victory. The expressed inability of two corps commanders to hold the positions assigned them occasioned its recall, and another move in the masterly retreat, before an army almost thrice the size of the Confederate force, effected in such good order that, as one of the General's staff remarked, "he had not left so much as a half grindstone north of the Etowah," a retreat, however, very discouraging, since it involved the surrender of the mountain fastnesses, the fall and destruction, by vandal torch, of Atlanta, and the unobstructed march of Sherman to the sea.

Our relief committee had gone to the front, in anticipation of a great battle, when, on the evening of the 19th instant, we received orders to fall back across the river. As the night drew on, and we sought to snatch a little sleep upon boxes and barrels, there mingled with the rumbling of the wheels the monotonous but pleasant tones of a boy's voice, that of a little drummer, perched upon the roof; and this was the ditty sung by him over and over again, with the ceaseless cadence of pounding feet:

"In eighteen sixty-one.
This war begun;
In eighteen sixty-four
This war will be o'er."

The song was history; it had nearly proved prophecy. In the winter of 1864 the Confederacy was almost in its death throes, and in the following spring a handful of war-worn veterans tearfully folded the Stars and Bars, and our chief yielded up his knightly sword with a dignity only equalled by the magnanimity of the victor.

For twelve years in succession I have had the pleasure of reading the annual addresses of Colonel Charles C. Jones, Jr., LL. D., President of the "Confederate Survivors' Association," of Augusta, Ga. I do not remember one which has not feeling sketches of some dead comrades who wore the gray. It reminds us of the rapidity with which the actors in those scenes, already covered by the obliterating waters of a quarter century, are "crossing the river," we trust, "to rest in the shade of the trees." Since this continent shook with the tread of armed hosts, a new generation has sprung into manhood and womanhood, to whom war experiences and plantation life are only traditions. It has occurred to one who had attained his majority before the tocsin of war summoned North and South to the field, and who, from birth, was intimately associated with that which was, at least, the *occasion* of the tremendous conflict, that a short series of letters upon the topic at the head of this article might not only prove pleasing to those who have had similar experiences, and interesting to those readers who were born since, or who were too young to have any distinct recollection of either war or plantation life in slavery times, but would, at the same time, subserve some graver and more important purposes, to be developed as we proceed. We shall have occasion to picture a civilization peculiar, and which can never be repeated in this country. Perhaps it will be seen that slavery, with all its confessed evils, was not "the sum of villainies," as some termed it, but had its redeeming qualities; that the common relations between master and slave were not of tyranny on the one side and of reluctant submission on the other; that our fathers, convinced that the institution was not in itself immoral, but scriptural, angered justly, and handicapped by the persistent efforts of Abolitionists to stir the slave even to insurrection, did much for the religious and mental elevation of their people.

The topics, subject to modification, and contraction or expansion, as necessity may require or mood suggest, that will be treated of, are: to state them as they now lie in the writer's mind, such as these-the writer's connection with slavery and slaves; the old plantation described; plantation occupations and sports; houses, food, physic, work, government, and family relations; Sacrament Sunday on plantation; "Daddy Jack," a curious character; a missionary to the blacks; anecdotes, mainly religious, of the negro; what the South did for his salvation and elevation; our First General Assembly and the negro; the slaves during the civil war, etc. Our letters will be brief, but, it is trusted, sufficiently full to accomplish the writer's purpose. May they, under God, result in renewing the kindly feelings which bound together the two races in the olden time, somewhat alienated, not simply by the results of the war, but by events since, which need not be named now, as they are past, let us hope forever. Possibly in the restoration of such feelings may lie at least an approximate solution of the race problem, now so deeply agitating the public mind.

CHAPTER II.
THE WRITER'S CONNECTION WITH SLAVERY
AND SLAVES.

IT was my lot from infancy to mid-life to have been intimately associated with that race whose premature enfranchisement wrought such temporary mischief in state, and whose present and future political and ecclesiastical status fills the hearts of statesmen and Christians alike with concern. I was the son of a well-to-do slaveholder, and myself, although never a planter, an owner at my marriage, by the generous gift of my father, of some of his trustiest and best servants, and also as trustee in my wife's right, and having our own servants always with us until emancipation.

The memories of that connection are of almost unmixed pleasure. In the interests of truth and candor, which I intend shall characterize these letters, I should here remark that at I saw slavery under its most favorable aspects. My home was in Liberty county, Ga., where that curse of Ireland, *landlord absenteeism*, did not exist, the planters, almost without exception, visiting their plantations during the summer at least twice a week, and spending the six months, including the winter, among them; in this county, too, at the period when my recollections of slavery began, our people had enjoyed for some time the apostolical labors of Rev. C. C. Jones, D. D., *nomen clarum et venerabile*. It is believed, however, that my experience will be found typical of the general experience; for while the congestion of the negro population in the rice and sugar districts, and measurably in some parts of the cotton belt, was accompanied by evils elsewhere unknown, it is believed that the great majority of this race were distributed into smaller bodies, in more direct contact with their masters.

As a babe, I drew a part at least of my nourishment from the generous breasts of a colored foster mother, and she and her infant son always held a peculiar place in my regards. A black nurse taught me, it is probable, my first steps and first words, and was as proud of both performances as the happy mother herself. With little dusky playmates, much of my holiday on the old plantation in the winter season was passed. Some parents were in this matter more particular than mine. On one plantation, I remember, the rule was that the white and black children were both punished if found playing together. My association with them was, I admit, somewhat to the detriment of my grammar, a fault which my schoolmaster speedily remedied, but never to the damage of my morals; for be it recorded, to their everlasting honor, while their words were sometimes coarse, they were rarely vulgar, and never profane. My experience may have been exceptional, but I do not remember, even among the adults, a single profane swearer!

With my little playmates I, as other children who are constantly rehearsing the drama of life, some times played at preaching; our pews, the leaf of a door set against the palings; three shingles, conveniently arranged, my pulpit; and a small book which I could not read, my Bible and hymn book; if the preaching was short and incoherent, the singing was neither. In my case this peculiar turn was not strange, for I bore the name of one of our pastors (the extent of the area occupied by the congregation during summer made the services of two necessary), and my father's plantation residence being next but one the nearest to the church, and he a prominent officer of it, was the preacher's home. In those days the old Midway church was known far and wide; and many is the Northern preacher visiting the South (not to say Southern) who found a warm welcome beneath the roof of our paternal mansion. Among them a frequent guest was the venerable octogenarian, Rev. Dr. McWhir, a polished Irish gentleman, finished scholar and learned divine, who had taught a school of which Washington was a trustee, and was the minister to whom the President apologized for returning thanks in his presence, replying to Mrs. Washington's remark, "My dear, you forget that there is a clergyman at the table;" "My dear, I wished him to know that I am not a *graceless* man." Here, too, winter after winter, was entertained Rev. Dr. Ebenezer Porter, of Andover Seminary, then admired all over the country, as much for the soundness as the solid attainments of its learned faculty. I remember to have heard my father say that Dr. P. was accustomed to observe that he always felt like taking off his hat in the presence of the grand old moss-covered live oaks, for which that region was and is noted.

At college, to which I went with the lively sympathy and good wishes of our people, I recall the faithful service of Uncle Peter, and at the seminary of Uncle Jack, not to speak of their wives. In the up-country, the titles of respect which Southern children were taught never to omit, were "Uncle" and "Aunty;" in the low country it was "Daddy" and "Maumma."

Coming events seem to have cast their shadows before them; for the child-preacher, when he came forth from the school of the prophets, began to preach to negroes in earnest, in their own special building (and a more appreciative and sympathizing audience he never has had); and in the old ancestral church, in which master and servant worshipped together, the colored people packing the wide, deep gallery, baptized from the same marble font, and taking the elements of bread and wine at the same time, from the silver baskets and gold-lined silver goblets, the gift of deceased slave-holders to the church. My first sole pastoral charge embraced a colored as well as a white membership, and among the former were some of my most consistent and valued members and attentive listeners. A regular Sabbath-school for them, children and adults, was taught by my young people, using Dr. C. C. Jones' Catechism, a manual prepared especially for them. And they also drilled them in hymns and tunes. Catechumens were carefully instructed by the young pastor in his own parlor, using the same manual as his basis. Besides preaching to them, where comfortable accommodations were provided in the common church, a weekly lecture, for which he made the same preparation which he did for the lecture to the whites, was delivered to full and most appreciative congregations, in a neat church building built for them by the trustees (all slave owners) of a benevolent fund, left to the county by a deceased slaveholder.

The unavoidable personal tinge given to this letter claims, as its justification, the necessity of establishing the competency and credibility of the witness.

CHAPTER III.

THE OLD PLANTATION.

IT was situated in rich lands, abounding in malaria, against which only the negro was proof. I remember an instance of a planter who had spent only one night on his plantation in this region, harvesting his corn, rendered desperately sick by it; and another, who lived in our village, dying from a high grade of bilious fever thus contracted. Consequently, the summer months were spent by the white families in what was known as "summer retreats," or villages located out in the pine forests; the return to the plantation was not considered safe until a killing frost had fallen.

How we children watched with our keen eyes and ears for the first signs which nature gave of winter's approach! What joy it was to see the yellowing leaves of the old china trees, which grew near the academies and old Union church, the poverty of the soil hastening the process; to feel the evenings growing cooler and cooler; to catch the first notes of "the six weeks' bird," which we implicitly believed always sang just that length of time before frost; to hear the woodman's axe, as he cut and split the great pine logs for the ordinarily unused fire-places of the summer home; and oh! the happiness to wake some bright morning and find the grass in the lawn all covered with mimic snow, and as we chased each other around the yard to mark the vapor pouring from our parted lips; we children called it "smoke!"

Word is sent down to the plantation-and not soon enough for our impatience-there come to move such furniture as we carried from one home to the other the double-horse wagon, and the two slow-moving ox-carts. Before we can get ready to start, Stingo, the old yard dog, a beast of exceeding ill-temper, aggravated by age, and, I am sorry to say, by the plaguing of his young master, to which his churlish disposition naturally exposed him, divining the cause of the unusual stir, set out by himself, and all alone made the journey of fifteen miles of good road, ready on our arrival to take charge of the family in their winter home.

Then the carriage and buggy are made ready, father, and mother, and children and nurse packed in, and we are, to our infinite delight, actually off at last for our winter holiday and the unspeakable joys of plantation life. On the way we halt at a clear spring, bubbling up by the roadside, and lunch, always, among other tempting edibles, upon shortened Johnny-cake! I wish it were in my power to give the housekeepers of our day the recipe; I only remember it was baked on a long clean board leaned before a wood fire, and was ambrosia to our healthy young appetites.

Resuming our journey along the broad, splendid roads, worked every fall by details of plantation laborers, under white supervision, we pass the old church where we shall worship anon, and of which more hereafter; drive along the wide Sunbury highway a half mile or more, and then turn at a right angle into our avenue, lined with live oaks, leading up to the plantation mansion. It is an unpretending structure, a large and roomy cottage of one and a-half storey, unpainted, a chimney of brick at one end, of clay at the other, a piazza running around two sides, and its gable end facing the avenue. It has only four glazed windows, two lighting the parlor, and the other two our parents' room just opposite, the panes small, and so imperfect that many is the time that our youthful imagination occupied itself, while waiting for the house-girl to kindle the fire in mother's chamber, in shaping its bubbles and defects into the images of different creatures. The parlor, the common living room, is papered with a pattern I have never seen elsewhere-a curious group of figures, which I see distinctly before me as I write. There is on the wide fireplace, with its fender and andirons, polished until you can see your face in them, a generous supply of oak and rich pine, but the big door leading out upon the piazza is persistently left open, I presume for ventilation, but bringing the sensations of freezing and burning into startling conjunction!

The arrangement of the houses is somewhat peculiar, but convenient, and apparently made upon the principle of placing everything as far as possible under the master's eye. Looking out from the front door, you see on your right the smoke and meat house, made of yellow clay, in which the bacon (for our planter raises or purchases his hogs from his own people) is cured and stored; on the left-hand corner, and in sight, is the kitchen, where French cooks are completely distanced in the production of wholesome, dainty and appetizing food; for if there is any one thing for which the African female intellect has natural genius, it is for cooking. Just over the palings of the front yard, you see the cotton houses, and directly in front the horse gin, with its wide branching arms carrying round and round all day the noisy rattling chain which turns the hickory rollers inside, with their lips separating the little black seeds from the fleecy lint, piling up in a growing bank of snow behind the screen. On the left, just beyond the stile (we called it the "blocks"), your eye takes in the stables and carriage-houses, and still farther away, and stretching to the left and in front, the single and double rows of cottages, the "quarters," the homes of the laborers, with their vegetable gardens, chicken coops, pig pens, rice ricks, and little store-houses. The only thing in the rear, and invisible from the front door, are the rice barns and winnowing house (for rice and Sea Island cotton constitute about in equal parts the market crop), and the vegetable garden, stocked with broad-headed cabbages in winter, and with its beds of fragrant chrysanthemums and the sweetest roses I have ever smelt! On every hand, the corn fields, with their brown stalks, and cotton fields with their leafless black bushes, stretching away to the encircling forests, and beyond them on the left the road leading by two tall sweetgums to the rice fields, great lakes now, and frequented by water fowl, and fringed with the dense moss-draped cypress swamps.

Such is a picture of the plantation home in which a large part of the sunny days of my childhood and youth were spent, and in immediate contact with the African race; and here for the present I close.

CHAPTER IV.
OCCUPATIONS AND SPORTS.

IT is not my intention to describe in this letter the ordinary work of a plantation, but only the occupations and amusements of the younger members of the planter's household.

Many of these were shared by the boys and girls of the family in their earlier years. These were, first, the almost daily visits to the cotton houses, where it was a pleasure to help the little slaves in beating up with switches the snowy cotton, as it lay upon the elevated scaffolding, airing in the winter's sunshine; or to take hold of the crank of the whipper, which, with its long revolving shaft, with numerous radiating spokes, separated the dust and trash from the cotton; and then to stand by the ginner and watch him, or be permitted for a few minutes ourselves to feed the grooved hickory rollers, as they draw in the fleecy cotton and divide the lint from the seed; or to supervise the packer, as suspended in his distended bag from the upper floor, with many a grunt, he, with his heavy pestle, forces the lint into the bale. Then what joy it was, in the keen winter's air, to perch upon the long beam outside, and travel miles and miles in a circle, ever-repeating itself, permitted as a special favor, for which a plate from the dinner table was exacted and willingly promised, and paid ourselves to drive the team.

At another time the barn-yard would be the special attraction, with its long parallel stacks of sheaves of golden rice. The dirt floor is beaten hard and swept clean, and the sheaves arranged upon it side by side; and now the stalwart laborers, with their hickory flails, beat off the heads of grain from the yellow straw; the obliging servants make for us children, or, if sufficiently skillful, we make ourselves, lighter flails, and, with our slighter blows, emulate in fun the heavier strokes of the men. And now the grain and broken straw are taken in baskets up the steps of the lofty winnowing house, which stands, stilt-like, upon its four upright posts; and as the grain and beaten straw are forced through a grated hole in the floor, the wind (faithfully whistled for) comes and carries off the chaff, and the round mound of rice steadily grows beneath. The rhythmical beat of the numerous flails is accompanied by a recitative and improvised song of endless proportions, led by one musical voice, all joining in the chorus, and can be heard a mile away, "The joy of the harvest," of which a Hebrew prophet speaks.

A spell of cold weather sets in, and now the well fattened hogs must be killed, dressed, and cured. We look on in the frosty air of the early morn, interested spectators, as the porkers are each dispatched by one dexterous blow of the axe, and then immersed in a cask of hot water to take off the hair, and aid in the trying up of the fat into lard and "cracklings," and, nothing loth, assist in the discussion at the family table of the spare-ribs and sausages; then there are horses to be ridden, and the difficult art acquired of keeping one's equilibrium upon the perilous edge of a frisky steed; then there are evening walks with our sisters up the long oak-lined avenue, and rambles through the encircling woods in pursuit of the black sloes and yellow haws and other winter berries. And then in early spring the cattle, turned out to graze in the fields and forests in the mild Southern winters, are to be hunted up and penned, and the young calves marked and branded; the latter operation performed by the cowherds, and the former furnishing ample field for the exercise of our newly-acquired horsemanship.

As we grow older, our sisters and us boys begin to separate in our pursuits for the most part. Now comes the savage age, the period of traps and bows and arrows; and many is the sparrow and robin brought home to our admiring sisters as trophies of our woodcraft and skillful marksmanship. From the Indian's implements, we are at last promoted to more civilized weapons, and actually (oh! height of a country boy's ambition!) own horse, saddle and bridle, dog and gun. Many now is the gray squirrel, and long-eared rabbit, and gentle-eyed dove, and plump partridge that falls under our new weapon. And, grown more ambitious, bird-shot is exchanged for duck and turkey-shot; and with my "man Friday" or boy "Dick" as inseparable companion, we are off for the rice-fields. In those days the teal and English ducks, as we called them, abounded in the two rice swamps between which the plantation was situated; and occasionally a flock of wild geese, to my intense excitement, settled down among them.

When frightened from their feeding-grounds by the passing of a wagon over the causeway bridges, or the sound of a gun, the water fowl took flight for a few minutes, to circle around and then to return, the noise of their wings was like that of a mighty rushing wind. The settlement of the Northern lakes, their breeding places even before I was grown, perceptibly diminished their numbers. Well do I remember the day when two fortunate successive shots brought me nine fat ducks, five of which I shouldered, leaving four for my faithful companion; and it was no light task to get them home. But I felt proud as Julius Cæsar decreed by the Roman Senate a triumph, and coming home from the war of Gaul or of Britain, when I passed the groups of servants about the cotton-houses and listened to their admiring comments. To secure these trophies I did not scruple, with my little comrade, to crush, barefooted and barelegged, a whole day through the thin ice which crusted the broad, overflowed rice fields, and suffered no harm. I was never tyrannical, as Southern boys generally were not, but sometimes a little positive and threatening in making Dick divest himself of pants, that he might cross some deep canal, which his young master did not care, with his rolled-up trousers, to attempt, to get his dead birds. Later on, duck and turkey-shot gave way to buckshot; but of that I will not now write, because it would take me into manhood.

Often I made adventurous voyages in the lake-like rice fields in my bateau, with its extemporized sail, and prudently provisioned with sweet potatoes roasted in a fire built on shore. Coffin shaped, when it was building in the street of "the quarters," the servants, as they came in from their work, with concern depicted in their faces, would ask, "Who is dead?" leading some of the family to predict that it would prove my coffin, which prediction, like many others as human, has proven false.

Then, when the dog-wood flower whitened the forests, came the spring fishing, Our rice fields were drained by wide, deep canals, stocked with various kinds of fresh water fish-trouts, mud-fish, cats, eels, chubs, perch (I give our names without vouching for their correctness). "Golden's drain" ("dreen" my black companions termed it,) was the canal oftenest visited, and with best results. I can remember to this day the very appearance of the different places where we broke our way through the sea myrtles to get the water's edge; and some positions inconveniently near the holes in the bank of two big alligators, male and female, which we had named.

Later in the season, as the waters became low, our negro men and boys "*churned*" for fish-a sport in which I sometimes shared. The operation was this: A flour barrel was taken, both ends knocked out, and the hoops secured; then a half-dozen boys and men, thus provided, would range themselves across a canal, and moving in concert, would each bring his barrel at intervals down to the bottom. The moment a fish was covered, its presence was betrayed by its beating against the staves in its efforts to escape; when the fisherman instantly covered his barrel with his breast, and with his hands speedily capturing it, threw it to the little negroes on the dam, who quickly strung it upon stripped branches of the sea myrtle tree. How they managed to handle the cat fish, with its sharp and poisonous spines, I cannot imagine; perhaps their horny hands were impervious to them, as they were to the live coals of fire which I have often seen them transfer with naked fingers from hearth to pipe; sometimes (an experience of which I have a lively personal recollection) a moccasin was covered, and then there was a rush to the shore, minus barrel.

As the rice fields later in the spring dried up in the heat, they left exposed the holes of the alligators-an animal which, more frequently than we liked, fed on uncured bacon, and occasionally docked, without improving her beauty, the tail of some thirsty cow. And now a long, lithe, slender pole is cut, its larger end furnished with a stout iron hook, and a negro man wading up to his waist in the water, feels with it until he touches the living occupant, when with a dexterous turn he fastens the hook under the alligator's foreleg, and now commences the tug of war! He is by main force dragged (in which operation other willing hands join) to the land, the pole allowed to turn with his revolutions as he comes to the shore, hissing like a goose. By a well-aimed blow of the axe, his head, with its formidable armature of teeth, is severed from its dangerous muscle, and his almost equally formidable weapon, his sweeping tail, is paralyzed. Sometimes, when unable to find the saurian, the pole is withdrawn; there are marks of teeth in startling proximity to the portion grasped by human hands! Well do I remember that, when somewhat callow, I would occasionally take to a tree until assured that the decapitation was a success!

It is easy to see how such a life, in which white and black, with the due subordination of master and servant preserved, shared the same sports, contributed to the familiar and affectionate relations which so notoriously from childhood bound master and servant together; and how it gave the Southern youth a skill with fire-arms rarely attained in a shooting gallery, and a free, firm, and graceful seat in the saddle, seldom if ever acquired in the sawdust arena of a riding school; and how it developed a splendid physical manhood, unknown to the dwellers in the cities, with their billiard table exercise and theatrical diversions, and what is at best but a poor substitute for outdoor sports, the gymnasium.

CHAPTER V.

THE NEGRO-HOW HE WAS HOUSED, FED, CLOTHED, PHYSICKED, AND WORKED.

IN this letter I shall speak, not without passing allusions to practices prevailing elsewhere, mainly of the general custom, with regard to the above matters, in my own native county; convinced that the representation will be recognized by the well-informed as a fair average picture of the conduct of the entire South.

The *houses*on some plantations were constructed of sawed lumber, furnished by the adjacent water-mills, or cut out by the negro sawyers laboriously, and not very accurately, with the whip-saw, worked in pen or pit, and making a tolerably fair joint possible. On our plantation they were, for the most part, covered with a weather-boarding of clapboards, split along the grain with what was called a frow, and from short cuts of cypress logs, and not admitting of a very close fitting. The houses were never lined within, so that only the thickness of a single board kept out the winter's air and cold. Usually the house had two or more unglazed windows, and a front and a back door, and was warmed by a clay chimney, with a wide hearth, abundantly supplied with oak and pine. You entered first the common living room. Separated from it, and with its door, was the family bedroom; and if the children were half-grown, you would find frequently one or two "shed-rooms," or *leantos*, in the rear, furnishing all proper privacy. The furnishing of the servants' home was primitive. There were a few benches and a rude rocker, all of home manufacture; shelves in the corner, containing neatly scrubbed pails and "piggins," made by the plantation coopers of alternate strips of redolent white cypress and fragrant red cedar, bright tins and white and colored plates, with the never absent long-necked gourd dipper, and beneath them the ovens, pots and skillets, the simple but most efficient paraphernalia of the mother cook.

The bedroom had a few boxes, containing the simple finery and Sunday clothes of the family; the week-day garments hung upon a string stretched across the corner; the bedstead consisted of a few boards nailed across a pair of trestles, and covered with the soft black moss so abundantly yielded by the adjacent swamps, and quite a number of good warm blankets, in which the sleepers, oblivious of change of seasons, would wrap themselves up, until not a square inch of sable skin was exposed.

Their *food* was mainly maize, which, where a public mill was handy, was ground for them; on my father's place they ground it themselves on the common hand mill; also the sweet potato, abounding in starch, the main nutritious ingredient in all food products; and easily and quickly cooked in the ashes, or baked before a fire. The weekly allowance for a "hand" or full worker was, I believe, a peck of corn, and four quarts additional for every child; and a half bushel of sweet potatoes to each adult, and to each child in same proportion. This weekly fare the year round was with us supplemented, in the season when the work was unusually heavy, by rations of molasses, or bacon, or salt fish; and an occasional beef. To this, thrifty servants added rice, of which they were as fond as the Chinese, and which they cultivated themselves in patches allotted them, and with seed and time afforded by their masters; and chickens and bacon of their own raising and curing, and fish of their own catching. So abundant were the rations of corn, that at the end of a week the careful house-holder sent quite a bag of it to the store to be exchanged for calico or tobacco!

As to their *clothing*, two good strong suits were given every year-in the summer, white Osnaburgs; in the winter, a kind of jeans, partly cotton and mostly wool, and stout brogans. The clothes were often cut and made up "in the big house" by negro seamstresses. The house-women were clad in a very neat fabric called "linsey woolsey," and with the house-boys fell heirs to the half-worn garments of the young masters and mistresses. A good warm blanket was given each worker every alternate year; so that a little care accumulated an abundance of warm bed covering.

As for their *physicing*, this was largely, and not unskillfully, done by the planter himself. In each plantation library was a book of medicine-my father's, I remember, was "Ewell's Practice"-books written without technical phrases, clearly describing, in the language of the common people, diseases and their remedies. As the maladies of the African, with his simple civilization, were rarely obscure, many planters acquired a very considerable skill in diagnosing and prescribing; and probably killed no more of their patients than the young M. D. graduate is said to kill, just in getting his hand in! A big jug of castor oil was always on hand, but it had to be kept under lock and key, so fond was the darkey of dosing himself for any and every ailment with that antiquated and heroic remedy; another thing he had the utmost faith in was the lancet; for, according to his simple therapeutics, it let the bad blood out; just as rubbing a sprained ankle with cold water toward the toes would send the inflammation from their tips into nothingness! When a case, however, was too serious or complicated, or obscure, for the planter's knowledge or skill, or obstinately refused to yield to the few remedies of his *materia medica*, Tom or Jerry was mounted on a swift horse and sent post haste for the doctor, five or ten miles away! Whenever we met a negro riding furiously, we always divined, "Going for the doctor," and were seldom wrong. He only checked up his foaming steed long enough to confirm our surmise, for it was his peculiar joy to tell the news, especially if bad. The doctor, it must be admitted, had but a poor chance either to cure or at his leisure to run up a bill, and this practice of only sending for his services in desperate cases depressed patient and doctor and nurses, and contributed sometimes to a fatal result. "To send for the doctor" was, in plantation belief, to give up the case; and the doctor's patients recovered only by a special miracle; but when they did not, they at least died *secundem artem*.

As for their *work*, they were never called out in the rain, and open sheds were always provided in distant fields against thunder showers. In some parts of the South they were, with an interval of a noon day rest of several hours, in the field from "sun up" to "sun down," but in all such instances their food was cooked for them, and they were generously fed upon full rations of bacon. With us the work was, in the main, extremely light. It was the duty of the men to split the pine rails with which the plantation was enclosed, to clear the forest from the "new ground" prepared for tillage. The women and the "thrash gang"-*i. e.*, the half grown boys and girls-made up the fences, the men commonly drove the plow, the women never handled anything thing heavier than the hoe; in the harvest both used the sickle, the men threshed the rice and trod the cotton foot-gin, while to the women was assigned the easier task of sorting the lint of its specks and leaves. Our lands were light and friable and easily worked, and for a large part of spring and summer the hands were allotted task work; and many is the time I have in the spring season seen the industrious laborer shouldering his hoe, with the sun high in the sky, ready to work his own allotted patch in the rice field, or to go "churning" or lounging and gossiping in the village street!

Compare the average house of the slave with the one-roomed mud hovel of the Irish tiller in Roman Catholic Ireland, with no privacy by day or night; the suitable and substantial clothing and bed covering supplied the slave with the scanty and sometimes ragged raiment of the poor in our great cities, and even laborers in our factories; their big fires, wood *ad libitum*, with the miserable, smouldering embers over which the poor sewing women crouch shivering in Northern cities; the excellent nursing and good medical attention given the slave, with the condition of many of the poor work-people, who dare not, or will not in their pride, call in a physician, for whose services they are unable to pay; compare hours of labor in the open air, not pushed to exhaustion and comparatively short, with the long and drastic work of many artisans, against which there is a constant demand for restrictive legislation; and add to this the consideration, that if the white master lived in comparative luxury upon the fruit of the labor of his slaves, he had all the care and forethought and responsibility of directing and organizing the labor for united efficiency; in a word, that he supplemented the African brawn with Anglo-Saxon brain; and it will be perceived *that no laboring population in the world were ever better off than the Southern slaves; and that there never was a falser accusation made against the Southern planter than this, harped upon by abolitionists of old, and repeated sometimes by Northern preachers now, that "he kept back the hire of the laborer."* The plain truth is just this, that *no tillers of the soil, in ancient or modern times, received such ample compensation for their labors.* He was not paid down, it is true, in cash, but he was amply compensated for his toil in free quarters, free medical attention, free food, free firewood, free support of sick, infirm, aged and young, and the free supply of that organizing faculty which utilized labor and made it more productive and capable of supporting, without the remotest fear of starvation, or even of scarcity, and without appeal to public charity, of entire slave communities, often as large as that of a good-sized village of whites!

CHAPTER VI.

THE NEGRO-NOW HE WAS GOVERNED.

IT was not unusual for defenders of slavery to describe the institution as patriarchal; it was undoubtedly such, but with some important modifications. Abraham was a nomad; he had no permanent connection with the soil, nor acquired more than a transient ownership by the digging of wells for his flocks; he had not a foot of it in actual possession, although all Canaan was, by divine gift, his, for his posterity. He did not sow and reap, as did his son Isaac. He was in no sense amenable to the laws of the land in which he temporarily sojourned with his family and flocks. His household, composed of his wives and servants "born in his house," or "bought with his money," constituted an independent commonwealth, of which he was the acknowledged sole and sovereign head; his will was law. On the contrary, the planter and his household were a part of the State. His slaves were recognized as in measure the basis of the electoral apportionment. They were, so far as capital offences were concerned, amenable to the laws of the country. If a negro committed murder, he was, by white and black testimony, and the verdict of a white jury, condemned, and by a white judge sentenced, and by a white sheriff hung. But all other offences, such as are now carried by them into a justice's court, were adjudicated by the master, from whose decision there was no appeal.

First, the *master* was the supreme authority on the plantation, in all matters but those in which human life was involved. Was a servant suspected of or caught thieving, or fighting, or beating his wife, he was summoned before the master, the witnesses heard, and justice, without appeal to innumerable authorities or the "law's delay," swiftly overtook the offender; the invariable penalty: so many lashes, according to the gravity of the offence. Over the house servants, the mistress had co-ordinate authority; indeed, the master seldom interfered in the domestic rule, save when called upon to assist. The sons and daughters of the planter also exercised a measure of authority, especially over the younger slaves, although they never, as a rule, were allowed to punish offenders.

Next to the planter in authority was the overseer. It was mainly upon large plantations, where the master needed aid, or where the plantation was owned by an unprotected female, or where the owner was habitually non-resident, that this important official was brought into requisition. He was usually a small planter, of acknowledged skill and experience and success, and ability to manage negroes. He usually lived on the place, in a house provided for him, getting a small salary in money, but allowed the use of horses, servants, food, and firewood. He was usually a man of family, and not infrequently saved enough to become in turn an owner of slaves and plantation. He exercised in the master's absence, authority over the slaves, with plenary power to punish offenders against plantation law and neglect of work, and his instrument was the lash.

Next to him stood the negro *driver*. Dr. C. C. Jones studiously avoided the use of this term, calling that official on his plantations the "foreman;" but in reality the term in Southern ears had no more suggestiveness of cruelty to men than the phrase "carriage-driver" has of cruelty to animals; and there was no more abuse of power ordinarily in the one case than in the other. The driver commonly carried what was known as a "cotton planter"-a short whip with heavy handle and tapering thong, plaited in one piece. It was usually worn around his shoulder, and was more a symbol of authority than an instrument of service; a reminder of the penalty of neglect than an implement of suffering.

Now, in regard to the actual exercise of this power and authority by planter, overseer and driver, we hesitate not to affirm that it was, in the main, as humanely administered as the imperfection of human nature permitted. As for the lash, it was used rarely upon the bare back, or excessively; and it should be remembered that it is only recently that flogging with the cat-o'-nine tails has been abolished in the navy. Although all intelligent slave-holders agreed with Dr. Thornwell, that all that the owner was entitled to was the reasonable service of the slave, and control of time and person only so far as was necessary to secure that end, there were undoubtedly masters who, at least in practice, seemed to assume that they owned their bodies as well as their service; masters who abused their authority to corrupt. I recall one instance now in the family of a favorite body-servant of my father, whose wife belonged to a wicked planter, although a professor of religion, in which, while only persuasion was used, the planter abused his position, with the consent of parents, to the ruin of a daughter; their insensibility to the sin and shame was to me the saddest part of the business. Then there were planters who were cruel. I recall in our county only two; the one a Southerner by birth. He flogged a slave to death! But the fellow-servants of his victim informed on him; the body was exhumed and their statements found correct, and upon their testimony and circumstantial proof he was, by a jury of indignant planters, sent to the Georgia penitentiary and ineffaceably branded as a felon. The other was a Northerner, and I remember to have heard the remark frequently made, that, while there were many honorable exceptions, as a general rule, the Northerners made the severest masters; and the explanation given was that they had not grown up with and formed attachments to the negro, and judged his capacity and energy by a white man's standard. This man was a member of our ancestral church; actually had his cook up before the Session for not making the full tale of waffles, as I have heard my father laughingly tell. He was so miserly withal that on more than one occasion he was known to direct a belated traveller to the minister's house as the village hotel, who, after "taking his ease at mine inn," and calling for all he wanted for man and beast, was, upon asking his bill next morning, astounded to find how he had been duped! He was also credited with opening his ditches on Sunday in a wet spell of weather-a thing unheard of in that Sabbath-observing community-and of rationing his servants in part on sour oranges! It was his practice to canter on his horse from slave to slave and whip them in the cotton rows! My father related that he once came unexpectedly upon him just emerging from the woods with an armful of young hickories; unable to hide them, he mumbled out an apology about "the aggravating character of negroes!" Well, his people killed him finally, as he deserved to be! Striking him in the head with the eye of a hoe, they saddled his horse, and, whipping him, sent him flying through the big gate and across the bridge to the town; and adroitly bloodying a knot which rose from one of the planks, they said that he had been thrown by his horse upon the bridge and instantly killed. Only a quarrel among them brought the killing to light a year after, when the body was taken up and examined and the story found correct. Several were convicted and hung. But I doubt not more sympathy was felt for the slave than the master. These were clearly exceptional cases, as rare, and no more indicative of general treatment of slaves than the conduct of the father who sat his child upon a red-hot stove to help him to recite the Shorter Catechism, is of the Northern Presbyterians' treatment of their children!

Humanity to slaves was secured by more than one influence. First, the Southern planter was as kindhearted and naturally philanthropic as any class of men found anywhere; then with us he was usually a college-bred man and of liberal culture. Not a few of them were as noble Christian gentlemen as were ever produced by any civilization; then there was a powerful public sentiment, which ostracized a cruel master. In addition to this, self-interest exercised a powerful influence in restraining from cruel treatment.

Injury to the slave was pecuniary loss. A curious illustration of the potency of this principle came under my observation in our civil war. Planters, who cheerfully surrendered their sons to the army, protested against the use of their slaves in the trenches! Then, above all, there was a strong attachment between the master and the servant, the natural result of closest association from childhood, which made cruelty foreign to the very nature of the owner.

As for the overseer, instances occur to me where the office was abused in both the directions just indicated. But these, again, were exceptional. The overseer usually enjoyed the protection of a family; wife and children throwing around him all the restraints of home life. He did not, perhaps, abuse his authority as a means of corruption, any more than the foreman of a factory; then, if cruel in his treatment, there was always the right of appeal to the owner. Convicted, the overseer received his "walking papers," his salary in full, with notice to leave as soon as he could get ready, and with a damaged reputation.

As for the negro driver, much the same line of remark applies to him. He was not sustained in his immorality, if he used his power to make life pleasant, or the reverse, to the women slaves to accomplish his purposes, and if cruel he was instantly deposed. The driver, the carpenter, the carriage driver and the house servant constituted the negro aristocracy. To be cast out of that favored circle of "the upper ten," was a disgrace almost more to be dreaded than death. There was all the dishonor in being "broken" as a driver, as it was termed, that there is in the army in being reduced to the ranks! It was by no means an unusual transaction, and occurred frequently enough to exercise a wholesome restraint upon the strong passions of the negro official.

In our next we shall treat of the marriage and family relations of the negro.

CHAPTER VII.
MARRIAGE AND FAMILY RELATIONS.

A HIGH officer of the Northern Presbyterian Church, Rev. Dr. Allen, Secretary of the Freedmen's Committee, in his *Quarter Century's Work Among the Freedmen*, affirms that when his church undertook their evangelization, "There was not a legal marriage among them, nor had been for two hundred years. A breach of the seventh commandment was no bar to church communion. Their religion was an enthusiasm rather than a principle, the enjoyment of religious worship depending chiefly upon the degree of animal excitement produced. To ignore the fifth, seventh, eighth and ninth commandments was not at all inconsistent with their idea of the religion of Jesus."

A slander, containing in it a measure of truth, is at once of the most offensive and dangerous kind. By it truth is dishonored, and error given what it does not in itself possess-vitality. Undoubtedly, there were not in slavery times marriages legalized by such formal documents as licenses, issued by competent courts; and the master had, under the law, the power of separating, by sale or removal, husband and wife; as this was a right supposed, whether correctly or incorrectly, to be incident to ownership. In too many instances the marriage relation was thus broken up, not often voluntarily but frequently providentially, by the death or bankruptcy of the master. But I have known instances in which the greatest sacrifices were made by humane masters to keep husband and wife together. Let me give an example or two occurring under my own observation. Harry Stevens was a very valuable slave, for he was a carpenter, pursuing his trade in Liberty and the adjoining counties, and paying his master a sure monthly and handsome wage, while laying by something for himself and family. His wife and family were freed by their master and sent to Liberia. My father, in order not to separate the family, sacrificed half his value, or about $750 or $900, and the balance was made up by contributions of neighboring slave-holders, and Harry became a citizen of the free African Republic! I have known planters also to hire hands they did not need, in order to keep husband and wife together. A service of this kind, which I had the opportunity of rendering to a favorite servant, was last summer gratefully recalled to my mind by his now aged widow.

The impression sought apparently to be made by the statement upon which we are animadverting is, that the marriage relation among the slaves was very loose and far from sacred. On the contrary, in our county not only was it gladly celebrated by the white pastor or colored minister, but, where they were preferred, by negro watchmen, who were appointed by the church as a kind of under-shepherds, and duly authorized to solemnize marriages. We hesitate not to say that the marriages thus contracted were, by the slaves themselves and their masters, generally regarded quite as sacred as marriages solemnized with legal license of the courts; and the obligations as commonly observed as among the same class anywhere. There were as many faithful husbands and wives, we believe, as are to be found among the working white population in any land.

The weddings of the house-girls were usually celebrated in the master's mansion-the bride decked for the altar by the skillful needles and elegant taste of the young mistresses of the household. On a large sugar plantation in Louisiana, owned by a distinguished Bishop of the Episcopal church, who fell near Marietta, Ga., fighting for the South, all the marriages were celebrated in the great house. The broad hall was decorated for the occasion with evergreens and flowers, and illuminated with many lights. The honor coveted by the white children, and given as the reward of good behavior, was to hold aloft the silver candlesticks as the good Bishop read the marriage service. If the couple had seriously misbehaved, they were compelled by the master to atone for it by marriage; and in that case there was no display, but the guilty pair were summoned from the field, and in their working clothes, in the study without flowers or candles, were made husband and wife.

On large sugar and cotton plantations marriages were not permitted with persons off the place. Even in such cases the choice was as wide as often falls to the lot of young white people living in a village community. In our county they were permitted to marry wherever they chose; and their almost universal choice was of husbands and wives at a distance from one to fifteen miles.

Saturday nights the roads were, in consequence, filled with men on their way to "wife house," each pedestrian, or horseman, bearing in a bag his soiled clothes and all the good things he could collect during the week, for the delectation of his household. Our cook, Maum Willoughby, used laughingly to say that before greeting Dublin, her husband, she always looked to see what he had brought in his bag for the family. This practice, of course, was not very good for family discipline; as the father was away from his child all the week, as indeed often occurs with white toilers everywhere, and they were left entirely to the management of the mother. Sometimes it made trouble on the plantation when the laborer came late to his Monday's task. It was, perhaps, due to this fact that news in our county spread like a prairie fire. The negro on his way to his family was as good as what was called in the war, "the grape vine telegraph."

The negro almost invariably married, and married young, for there were no costly preparations to be made, no ambition of bride for a palace to be consulted.

A house was speedily erected by the plantation carpenter for the newly-married pair; as for food, raiment and medicine, that was the master's concern. I remember now but two negro bachelors, and I believe they only remained in single blessedness for a season. Of course, we would not hold them up as model parents; this they were not, and only too much disposed to resort to blows and slaps in family matters. But they were neither better nor worse, perhaps, than the working class of any country.

As for the strange intimation, that violations of the seventh commandment were no bars to church communion in Southern churches, it is simply, so far as my acquaintance with the subject warrants positiveness of statement, notoriously and injuriously false. Two facts will be enough to prove this averment. In our county-and I suppose it was largely true elsewhere-the most frequent cause of suspension from church fellowship, and even excommunication, was offences against identically this commandment; and then, farther, while here and there, especially in the cities, were churches composed entirely of negroes, members and officers, such exclusive organizations were, as a matter of policy and safety, discouraged generally at the South. As a rule, the churches of the South had a mixed membership, white and black; and if they had a negro preacher, he was usually under the control of the white pastor. To insinuate, then, that violations of the seventh commandment were, in the South, in slavery times, no bars to church communion, is to charge the white Christians of that section with a criminal complicity, which only a complete array of well-attested facts can redeem the author of the libel from the accusation of a wilful bearing of false witness against his neighbor. (Ex. xx.16.)

CHAPTER VIII.
"DADDY JACK."-A CURIOUS CHARACTER.

I WISH I had the genius of a Dickens, so skillful in portraying life among the lowly, that I might do justice to the odd creature whose name heads this letter. I suppose that he must have been born (most people are), although I do not remember having ever heard of his parents. Kindred he seemed to have none-neither brother nor sister, uncle, aunt, nor cousin; but he was one all to himself. A glance at his face would have convinced you that if ever the slightest strain of white blood mingled with the African current, it must have effected a junction with it before the confusion of tongues at Babel, when, as some ethnologists suppose, a diversity of races was miraculously produced. When I first recollect him, he had attained to middle life.

"Daddy"-the title of respect low-country children of Georgia were taught to give every elderly man servant- "Daddy Jack" was a queer negro. For example, he was mostly a bachelor. Single blessedness was so uncommon among the slaves, and for a reason already mentioned-the absolute easiness and certainty of the support of a family- that I now recall but two bachelors in my large acquaintance among them; and one of these, I learned last summer in a visit to my native county, had finally surrendered to the charms of the other sex, and, I believe, died in the yoke. Daddy Jack was a Benedict once, and for a short time. How it happened I am not able to say; whether it was leap-year or not I am not advised; but "Maum Nanny," a widow, ensnared him. My impression is she did most, if not all, of the courting, and the all-prevailing argument was her ability to cook a nice pot of hominy, or, better still, a savory mess of rice, and skillfully to bake a hoe cake!

Their honeymoon must have been a tempestuous one, for, as the negroes were accustomed to express it, "they divided blankets,"perhaps, before the next "full of the moon." Nor was this to be wondered at, for he was, like Rip Van Winkle, a shiftless, good-natured fellow; but, unlike him, full of oddities that did not minister to a wife's comfort He was at once the idlest and the most industrious slave on the plantation; indolent where his own interests were concerned, active where his master's were affected.

I recall now the report of one of my dusky playmates, of what he had just seen and heard, and in his lingo: "As I bin gwine long de street, and pass Buh Jack house, I yeddy somebody duh whistle, and I look in de door and I see Buh Jack a sitten on de jice and pullin' down de shingles to make fire wid!"

Most of our readers have heard of the Arkansas traveller, who, accosting a man playing on his fiddle beside the door of his ruined cabin, with the question, "Friend, why don't you mend your roof," receives (the bow suspended only for a minute for the purpose) this answer: "When the sun shines, I don't need to, and when it rains I can't." Daddy Jack made the leaks with his own hand, and ran the risk of a wetting to insure a warming! From the same authority, I also learned that a straw hat which my father had given him had been used by the improvident fellow in kindling the fire.

My father had a great fondness for him, and gave him two suits of clothing where the rest received one; and a blanket every year, instead, as was common, every alternate year; but as he was unaccustomed to the use of thimble and needle, and generally had no wife or sister to mend for him, his clothing was not always presentable; his newest blanket was speedily in holes from a habit he had. In his room (parlor, chamber, and kitchen, all in one), I do not remember to have seen any sleeping accommodations. I doubt if he ever undressed and went regularly to bed; his habit was to rake aside the fire coals and then spread his blanket upon the ashes of the hearth, where he could feel its grateful warmth. Whether he temporarily altered his sleeping habits upon the advent of his bride, we cannot say, but think it doubtful.

I have read of some race that, by a singular inconsistency, are nice about their persons, but not cleanly about their clothing. Our friend, perhaps, never washed his garments, and he had no female friend to do it for him, but he was a diligent bather. At midnight, in mid winter, he would divest himself of all his clothing, and plunge into the "calf-hole," an excavation made to contain water for the younger cattle.

Almost too idle to cook his own food, he would, as my playmates laughingly said, "work all day for one spoonful of hominy!" I have often heard him at the hand-mill long before I, an early riser, was up, grinding corn for some trifling reward.

My father gave him, as he did the rest of the people, a piece of good land to cultivate in rice, of which he was as fond as any Chinaman, and provided the seed; well, he had to order the driver to flog him to make him turn up the soil; and then he defeated the master's kind design by beating out the rice and planting his plot with the chaff.

I never knew him to be sick for a day, and he was never behind-hand in his tasks, and never punished for idleness where his master's work was concerned.

With all, Daddy Jack was a professing Christian, and called himself a Presbyterian; but, as like as not, he had not the first conception what the word meant, except that it signalized the fact that he once "jined" Midway Church, and not Newport, the Baptist, and had been sprinkled and not dipped. He was, no doubt, regular in attendance upon plantation prayers, and sung loudly, when not asleep, and sometimes when he was; and was always in his place at church, especially "Sacrament Sunday." Daddy Jack had a profound conviction of the reality of both heaven and hell. He was very sure two people of his acquaintance were bound for the better of the two-"Old Miss and Mass William." "He knew their calling and election" by this token, the generous plates of victuals they were accustomed to send the faithful servant from their tables. Perhaps he had scriptural ground for this persuasion; for was he not one of the "little ones" to whom "the cup of cold water," or its more valued cup of hot coffee, "was given in the name of a disciple," and one of the hungry brethren whom they had fed and concerning whom the Master would say, "Inasmuch as ye have done it unto one of the least of these my brethren, ye have done it unto me."

The death of my honored parents-the one scarcely disturbed in her last hours by the guns of Fort Sumter; the other, after a few weeks, on the next national anniversary, following the companion of fifty years' happy wedded life into the Beyond-caused a division of property, and Daddy Jack passed to one of my married sisters in the same county.

The war went on, and I removed to a distant part of the State, and after it to Louisiana, and so I lost sight of Daddy Jack for a time, but I hope some day to meet the dear old shiftless, good-natured, harmless fellow in the better land, where all that was defective in his organization and character will have been removed.

Recently I heard a colored bishop of the Methodist Church exclaim, in an earnest address: "Some ask, 'will we have the same color in heaven we have had on earth?' This I do not care to know; all I wish is to make sure of getting there, and not being barely saved, but going 'sweeping through the gates.' "

We cannot tell what changes will be effected at the resurrection in the bodies of the saved; but some of the whitest souls I have ever known dwelt in the blackest of skins! Perhaps, and if some commentators are correct, certainly, if color, as well as servitude, was a part of the curse denounced upon Canaan for the sin of Ham, it will be changed. But this we do know, that nothing will sever the chain of holy love which in heaven will forever bind heart to heart, and all to the God of love; for hear the beloved John: "After this I beheld, and lo! a great multitude, whom no man could number, of all nations and kindreds and tongues, stood before the throne, and before the Lamb, clothed with white robes, and palms in their hands." And to him the angel makes answer concerning them: "These are they which came out of great tribulation, and have washed their robes and made them white in the blood of the Lamb."

CHAPTER IX.

FOLK LORE OF THE NEGRO.

FOLK lore, transmitted orally from sire to son-. constituted the only literature of the negro slave, who, as a rule, was unacquainted with the alphabet of his master.

Here I hope I may be permitted, in accordance with the general spirit and tenor of these letters which are designedly and largely the testimony of one who narrates what he has seen and heard, to recall some childhood experiences. Before we were considered old enough to attend evening religious services, we children were left at home in charge of the house servants, who were accustomed to entertain us by the relation of negro fables.

Not a few Southern writers, notably our own Ruth McEnery Stuart, have, in the field of fiction, correctly portrayed both negro character and dialect; the author named, with a pathos and sympathy with her lowly subjects, which often exacts from those who knew the negro before emancipation the involuntary tribute of tears: but only two of them have wrought in the rich field of the negro folk lore-Joel Chandler Harris and Charles C. Jones, Jr. The fables related by these last mentioned writers were, in the main, those recounted at the planter's fireside to the never weary youthful auditors. With Joel Chandler Harris's recitals, the thousands of the readers of the *Century* have been made familiar in the narratives of "Uncle Remus;" not so many have perused the account of them in a little book from the press of Houghton, Mifflin & Co., entitled, "*Negro Myths from the Georgia Coast, told in the vernacular,*" by Charles C. Jones, Jr., LL. D. Reared in the same community with the latter author, I desire to testify to its literal accuracy in story and dialect. There is not a particle of fiction in either. I learned from him that they were taken down from the lips of old negroes in Liberty county, Ga. The dedication of this little volume is characteristic, but will be no surprise to those who had any knowledge of domestic service in the South before emancipation: "In memory of Monte Video Plantation, and of the family servants, whose fidelity and affection contributed so materially to its comfort and happiness."

Let me again bear my testimony as one who was by marriage, a frequent visitor, and for weeks at a time, a fortunate resident beneath the roof which sheltered the ""Apostle to the blacks," and the author who, as his eldest born, bears his father's honored name, in one of those typical Southern homes, in which polish and culture were combined with piety, to the fact that these family servants were all that the dedication of their once young master portrays them to have been.

Between these stories of two authors, there is, as might have been expected, some sameness, as they were conscientious workers in the same general field; but a perceptible variation in their versions and dialect, due to the fact that they wrought in different parts of it-Mr. Harris giving the dialect and folk lore of the negroes of middle Georgia, and Mr. Jones those of the negroes of the coasts of Georgia and of South Carolina.

As the seaboard was first settled and supplied with African labor, it is evident that the fables preserved and recorded by the latter author have the preference as the originals. I have, in my partial investigations, been astonished to find how far these fables have spread into the interior, and how, with natural and, in some instances, most amusing variations, they have been transmitted by tradition with substantial correctness. President George J. Ramsey, of Silliman Collegiate Institute, Clinton, La., tells me that in the last years of the war, he, as a child, heard "Uncle Remus" fables in East Virginia; and our servant man, who was a Federal soldier in the war, gives me substantially the story of the Tar Baby at the Well, as told in *Negro Myths*, but with a laughable variation in its ending-perhaps a Louisiana addition.

I will now, from the fifty-seven originals collected by Charles C. Jones, Jr., give two specimens:

BUH SQUIRLE AND BUH FOX.

Buh Squirle bin berry busy duh gedder hickry nut on de groun fuh pit away fuh feed heself and eh fambly der winter time. Buh Fox bin er watch um, and befo Buh Squirle shum, eh slip up an graff um. Buh Squirle eh dat skaid eh trimble all ober, an eh bague Buh Fox let um go. Buh Fox tell um, say eh bin er try fuh ketch em long time, but he hab sich sharpe yeye, an keen yez, an spry leg, eh manage fuh dodge um; an now wen he got um at las, eh mean to fuh kill um an eat um. Wen Buh Squirle find out dat Buh Fox yent bin gwine pity um an tun um loose, but dat eh fix fuh kill um and eat um, Buh Squirle say to Buh Fox: "Enty you know say, nobody ought to eat eh bittle befo eh say grace ober um?" Buh Fox him mek answer: "Dat so;" and wid dat, eh pit Buh Squirle een front er um, an he fall on he knee, an kibber eh yeye wid eh han, an eh tun een fuh say grace.

While Buh Fox bin do dis, Buh Squirle manage for slip way; an wen Buh Fox open eh yeye, eh see Buh Squirle duh run up de tree way him couldn't tetch him.

Buh Fox fine eh couldn't help ehself, an eh call arter Buh Squirle, an he say: "Nummine boy, you done git way now, but de nex time me clap dis han topper you, me giune eat you fus and say grace arterward."

Best plan fuh er man fuh mek sho er eh bittle befo eh say tenkey fur um!

BUH WOLF, BUH RABBIT, AN DE TAR BABY.

Buh Wolf and Buh Rabbit bin nabur. De dry drout come. Ebry ting stew up. Water scace. Buh Wolf dig one spring fuh git water. Buh Rabbit him too lazy an too schemy fuh wuk fuh isself. Eh pen pon lib off tarruh people. Ebry day when Buh Wolf yent duh watch um, eh slip to Buh Wolf spring, an eh fill him calabash long water, an cah um to eh house fuh cook long and fuh drink. Buh Wolf see Buh Rabbit track, but eh couldn't ketch um duh tief de water.

One day eh meet Buh Rabbit in de big road, an ax um, how eh mek out fuh water. Buh Rabbit say: "Him no casion fuh hunt water; him lib off de jew on de grass." Buh Wolf quire: " Enty yuh blan tek water outer my spring?" Buh Rabbit say: "Me yent." Buh Wolf say: "You yis, enty me see you track?" Buh Rabbit mek answer: "Yent me gwine to your spring, mus be some udder rabbit; me nebber been nigh you spring; me dunno way you spring day."

Buh Wolf no question um no more; but eh know say eh bin Buh Rabbit fuh true, an eh fix plan fuh ketch um.

De same ebenin, eh mek tar baby, an eh guine, an set um right in de middle er de trail wuh lead ter de spring an dust in front er de spring.

Soon a mornin, Buh Rabbit rise and tun in fuh cook he bittle. Eh pot biggin fuh bun. Buh Rabbit say: "Hey! my pot duh bun. Lemme slip to Buh Wolf spring an git some water fuh cool um." So he tek eh calabash and hop off fuh de spring. When eh ketch de spring, eh see de tar baby duh stan dust een front er de spring. Eh stonish. Eh stop. Eh come close. Eh look at um. Eh wait fur um fuh move. De tar baby yent notice um. Eh yent wink eh yeye. Eh yent say nuttin. Eh yent mobe. Buh Rabbit, him say: "Hey, Titer, enty you gwine tan one side and lemme get some water? " De tar baby no answer. Den Buh Rabbit say: "Leely gal, mobe, me tell you, so me kin dip some water outer de spring long my calabash." De tar baby wunt move. Buh Rabbit say: "Enty to know my pot duh bun? Enty you yeddy, me tell you fuh mobe? You see dis han? Ef you don't go long an lemme git some water, me guine slap you ober!" De tar baby stan day. Buh Rabbit haul off an slap um side de head. Eh fastne. Buh Rabbit try fuh pull eh hen back, an eh say: ""Wuh you hole me han fuh? Lemme go. Ef you don't loose me, me guine box de life outer you wid dis tarrah han." De tar baby yent crack eh teet. Buh Rabbit hit him bim wid dis tarrah han. Dat han fastne too, same luk tudder. Buh Rabbit say: "Wuh you up teh? Tun me loose. Ef you don't leggo me right off, me guine knee you." De tar baby hole um fast. Buh Rabbit skade an bex too. Eh faid Buh Wolf come ketch um. Wen eh fine eh can't loosne eh hen, eh kick de tar baby wid eh knee. Eh knee fastne. Yuh de big trouble now. Buh Rabbit skade den wus dan nebber. Eh try to fuh skade de tar baby. Eh say: "Leely gal, you better mine who you fool long. Me tell you fuh de las time, turn me loose! Ef you don't loosne me han and me knee right off, we guine bust you wide open wid dis head." De tar baby hole um fast. Eh yent say one wud. Den Buh Rabbit butt de tar baby een eh face. Eh head fastne same fashion luk eh han an eh knee. Yuh de ting now! Po Buh Rabbit dune for! Eh fastne all side. Eh can't pull loose. Eh gib up. Eh bague. Eh cry. Eh holler. Buh Wolf yeddy um. Eh run day. Eh hail Buh Rabbit:

"Hey, Budder, wuh de trouble? Enty you tell me you no blan wisit my spring fuh git water? Who calabash dis? Wuh you duh do you any how?" But Buh Rabbit, so condemn, he yent hab one wud fuh talk. Buh Wolf him say: "" Nummine, I dune ketch you dis day. I guine lick you now!" Buh Rabbit bague. Eh prommus nebber fuh trouble Buh Wolf spring no more. Buh Wolf laugh at um. Den he tek an lose Buh Rabbit from de tar baby, en eh tie um teh one sparkleberry bush, an git switch an eh lick um til eh tired. All de time Buh Rabbit bin a bague an holler. Buh Wolf yent duh listne ter him, but eh keep on duh pit de lick ter um. At last Buh Rabbitt tell Buh Wolf: "Don't lick me no mo. Kill me one time. Make fire and burn me up. Knock my brains out gin de tree!" Buh Wolf mek answer: "Ef I bun you up, ef I knock you brains out, you guine dead too quick. Me guine trow you in de brier patch, so de briers can cratch you life out." Buh Rabbit say: "Do, Buh Wolf, bun me, brake me neck, but don't trow me in de brier patch. Lemme dead one time. Don't terrify me no mo."

Buh Wolf yent know wuh Buh Rabbit up the Eh tink eh bin tare Buh Rabbit hide off. So wuh eh do? Eh loose Buh Rabbit from the spakleberry bush. and eh tek um by de hine leg an eh swing um roun, an trow um way in de tick brier patch fuh tare eh hide, and scratch eh yeye out. De minnie Buh Rabbit drap in de brier patch, eh cock up eh tail, eh jump, an holler back to Buh Wolf: "Good bye, budder! Dis de place me mammy fotch me up!" and eh gone befo Buh Wolf kin ketch um. Buh Rabbit too schemy.

The first of these fables, in the raciness of its wit, equals anything in Æsop.

To the other, our Louisiana negro man contributes this amusing variation as its close, which also illustrates the "scheminess" of Buh Rabbit:

"Buh Bear comes along and finds Buh Rabbit in the involuntary embrace of 'the leely gal,' the tar baby, and inquires as follows: 'Hey! Buh Rabbit, wat you duh da?' Says Buh Rabbit, moving to and fro as far as his imprisoned members will admit: 'Oh, I duh see-saw; wouldn't you like to see-saw, Buh Bear?' 'Yes,' says Buh Bear, in his innocence. 'Well, pull me off and you git on.' Buh Rabbit released, Bruin takes his place; and while stuck fast is taken for the thief. Buh Rabbit takes himself off; and Buh Wolf beats Buh Bear almost to death!"

These stories are almost entirely and purely fables-that is, narratives in which animals are endowed with speech; only to a very limited degree do human beings figure in them. They are never, except in the remotest sense, religious, and seldom, if ever, rise above the level of the ethics of Benjamin Franklin's proverbs. If any criticism is proper from a moral standpoint, I should say that they, or some of them, glorify cunning and falsehood at the expense of honesty and truth, but in such a way that we cannot but laugh at the story, while we withhold our admiration from its teachings. It is also a curious fact that (for what reason we are at a loss to say) the Rabbit is the embodiment of smartness, and not the Fox, the Anglo-Saxon's model of cunning, and who, by the way, in the story quoted, is outwitted by the Squirrel.

The literary world is greatly indebted to the two Georgia authors named, for rescuing from the incoming tide of oblivion, which is fast obliterating all that was peculiar in the past civilization of a people who were the innocent cause of the bloodiest and most transforming war of modern times. For, strange to say, and I now speak from the testimony of the author of "The Negro Myths," who found much reluctance in communicating them, and from my own observation in the case of a negro woman whom I had raised, that not only are the new ideas engendered by freedom supplanting this folk lore, but the religion as now taught among them by their colored preachers is setting itself against their narration as sinful. They did not perceptibly harm the morals of Southern children, black or white, and were infinitely preferable to the blood-curdling ghost stories with which some nurses terrify the young in our day. They are certainly, in the matter of injurious influence, not to be compared to the dime novels, to which the almost universal acquisition of the art of reading gives our young Africans unrestricted access.

CHAPTER X.
OLD MIDWAY-A TYPICAL CHURCH.

IT was remarked in a previous letter that the Southern churches, with a few exceptions, had a mixed membership; that is, were composed of whites and blacks, the whole being under the government of the former. In this respect, the Midway church was a typical church. It had a membership of perhaps five hundred, about three-fourths of whom were negroes.

The church edifice, which was situated in Liberty, one of the seaboard counties of Georgia, thirty miles southwest of Savannah, was called "Midway," because equi-distant between the two great rivers-the Savannah and the Alatamaha. It was central to a very rich but malarial region, whose original growth was cane, oak, hickory and cypress.

Bearing in colonial times the name of "St. John's Parish," the county received by legislative enactment shortly after the Revolution, the honorable title of "Liberty," in commemoration of its plucky conduct in taking decided measures to join the other colonies in their revolt, when the Provincial Council of Georgia had refused to unite with them! It is a remarkable and noteworthy fact, that a county which perhaps never had more than between two or three thousand whites, had thus the honor of contributing two signatures to that immortal document, the Declaration of Independence-Lyman Hall and Button Gwinnett.

Made rudely acquainted in earlier times with the torch and tomahawk of the savage, it was her destiny in the Revolution, as more recently in our civil war, to know the baptism of fire and blood. Col. Prevost, of the British Army, burned the rice in stacks, and some of the houses of the planters, and reduced to ashes the sacred edifice in which they had worshiped the God of their fathers. General Screven was killed not far from the church site. Col. McIntosh, one of her gallant sons, who commanded the small earthen redoubt protecting her flourishing little seaport of Sunbury, at the mouth of the Midway, to the demand of Col. Fuser, of unconditional surrender, returned the laconic reply:

"Come and take it!"-an invitation finally and prudently declined by the commander of his Majesty's forces? When Washington visited Georgia in 1791 the "Congregational Church and Society at Midway" presented to him a patriotic address, to which the Father of his Country made a fitting and handsome reply.

This early and ardent espousal of the cause of the revolting colonies by the church and society of Midway is, perhaps, to be accounted for by the naturally stron gties which still bound them to New England. Their ancestors came from Britain to secure liberty of worship, and first settled not far from what is now the city of Boston, at an Indian town, which, in honor of the native place of some of the settlers, and of a cherished minister, they called Dorchester. Sixty years afterwards their descendants, largely influenced by religious motives, moved as a church, with their pastor, Rev. Joseph Lord, a Congregational minister, to South Carolina, and settled on the Ashley river, about eighteen miles above Charleston. This settlement they also called Dorchester. After a residence of more than fifty years, finding their lands impoverished and insufficient for themselves and descendants, and somewhat discouraged by their continued unhealthiness, they again emigrated in a body, under their pastor and officers, to Georgia, and effected a settlement in a district at the headwaters of the Midway and Newport rivers, two short tide-water streams, draining what is now known as Liberty county. Coming to this wild country as a church, they secured from the colonial government a large tract of land, compactly situated; and by articles of agreement the colonists pledged themselves not to alienate any of their land to outsiders, save with the unanimous consent of the society. They speedily built a neat church, or "meeting-house," as it is called in the records, "at the cross-paths," at a point central to the settlement. Their first pastor at least was a Congregational minister, and the government of the church somewhat peculiar. It was not purely Congregational; for the control of church matters was not in the hands of the whole society, but of a session, composed of all the male members, without respect to age. Their officers were deacons and a body of "select men" as they were called. Every year the church went through the routine of electing a pastor. Retaining this nondescript form of church government down to our late war, the church has from early times been served by Presbyterian ministers only, and its members have always regarded themselves as Presbyterians.

Puritan by ancestry, they were a pre-eminently godly people; first in their estimation was the church, and next the school-house. The Sabbath was strictly observed. One of the church officers was also justice of the peace. Should some traveler attempt to pass on the Lord's day with his wagons and teams on the public highway, running by the church, he was by this zealous administrator of law, human and divine, peremptorily halted; but then taken home with him and freely and most hospitably entertained, he and his beasts, and on Monday sent on his way rejoicing, with a hearty Godspeed!

The Westminster Assembly's Shorter Catechism was diligently taught in all its families. Celebrating some time before the late war its centennial, this remarkable church (not to exhaust the roll-call of its worthies) has furnished more than one theological professor, such as Rev. Drs. Thomas Golding and C. C. Jones; forty ministers of the gospel, not a few of whom have been eminent for their talents and piety, for example, Rev. Dr. Daniel Baker; a number of distinguished physicians and college professors, not a few of them known in the scientific world, as for instance, Dr. Joseph Jones, of New Orleans, and the brothers Le Conte, of California. It has given eminent men to the bar, such as Judge Law, late of Savannah, Col. C. C. Jones, Jr., LL. D., of Augusta, Ga., and others; it has supplied teachers by the hundred, and has trained (only the judgment can reveal how many) a multitude of saved sinners for heaven, and by her liberal gifts of means and of men, like Way and Quarterman, to foreign missions, has helped to extend the kingdom of our Lord and Saviour in the world.

The war wrote "*Finis*" on the last page of this remarkable and honorable history. The changed relations of master and servant have consolidated the blacks in this region, and scattered the whites into the remoter and healthier parts of the county. A colored Presbyterian church, under a white pastor, and in connection with the Northern Assembly, are now the only worshipers in the sacred edifice-built in 1790. It is now, by permission of the descendants of the white members, used by the negroes, upon the easy terms of keeping in good order the adjacent graveyard," in which repose the ashes of four or five godly generations. *It is a church with a finished history!* But as her sons and daughters, inheriting the sterling piety of their fathers, gather annually upon this hallowed ground to lovingly commemorate the historic past, they illustrate in their own persons, characters, and celebration, the blessed fact that the gracious influences set in motion by an earnest Christian church, continue even when, in the providence of God, it, as an organization, has become extinct.

And the history of this venerable church, so briefly sketched by one of her loyal and loving sons, it seems to him, is but a providential comment upon those sweet words of Moses: "Know, therefore, that the Lord thy God, he is God, *the faithful God, which keepeth covenant and mercy with them that love him and keep his commandments, to a thousand generations.*"(Deut. vii. 9.)

In our next letter we shall attempt to draw from memory a picture of "Sacrament Sunday in old Midway church."

CHAPTER XI.

SACRAMENT SUNDAY AT OLD MIDWAY

"THE sacraments of the New Testament are Baptism and the Lord's Supper," says the Shorter Catechism, which contains in brief the creed of this ancient church, and which was diligently taught their children. Both were commonly administered on communion Sabbath, for seldom did the day pass without numerous additions of white and black, the latter almost invariably receiving adult baptism. But it is probable that it was the Supper that was mostly in the mind of our forefathers, when they called communion Sabbath, occurring four times every year, "Sacrament Sunday."

It was a great day with both white and black, and anticipated with joy by the pious, and interest by all. There was a peculiar quiet about the morning of the sacred day on the plantation. All the sounds of the busy week have ceased; the noisy rattle of the chain of the horse gin is silent., the flails in the barnyard are still; few loud calls are heard about the quarters; the negroes are seen sitting on the sunny sides of their houses, mothers with their children's heads in their laps, carrying on in public an operation better suited for in-door privacy; no sounds are heard but the lowing of the cattle, the whinnying of the horses, the crowing of the cocks and cackling of the hens; the gobbling of the turkeys; the shrill cries of the geese; the winds appear to be asleep, and the very sunshine seems to fall more gently than during the week upon the widely extended fields and surrounding woods!

Our honored father, a deacon of the church, sits by the window, and with a knife carefully sharpened the day before divides upon a clean white board the wheaten loaves into little cubes of bread, and the "elements," as they are called, together with the genuine silver goblets and silver tankards and silver baskets, previously polished by the deft hands of the house girl, with the little contribution boxes for the offering in aid of the poor, are all safely packed away in a wide basket.

Prayers and breakfast over, the family dress for church; and now the order is sent out to the stable boys and the carriage driver to "harness up;" and directly the high-pitched carriage, with its lofty driver's seat and swinging between its "C"springs, and the two-wheeled "top-gig" and the saddle horses are brought around to the front gate; and although it is scarcely more than nine o'clock, and the distance "a short mile," the entire family, as was the custom, ride to church. As we roll along the broad highway, we find the servants clean and neatly dressed and in their best, some on foot and others in Jersey wagons, crowded to their utmost capacity with little and big, and drawn by "Marsh Tackey's," equal in bottom and strength to, and no larger than, Texas ponies-all moving in the same direction; those on foot carrying their shoes and stockings in their hands, to be resumed after they shall have washed in the waters at the causeway near the church; for they believe in treading the Lord's courts with clean feet! Many are the kind greetings and mutual inquiries after the health of each other and of their families, exchanged by whites and blacks.

We are among the first to arrive, but every moment we hear the thunder of vehicles rolling across the half dozen bridges of the swamp causeway near at hand, and the neighing of horses; and here come the multitude, from distances of from one to ten miles and more. Horses are unharnessed and secured, and the worshipers fill the small houses surrounding the church, or stand in the sunshine, or saunter about the grounds, or visit the "graveyard."

Under my father's superintendence, the long narrow red-painted tables and benches are brought out from the vestry and carried into the church, and arranged in the aisle before the pulpit. The church building, 40x60 feet in size, is very ancient; it was built in 1790; it is the successor of one destroyed by the British, and of a plainer and coarser put up after the Revolution. It is of wood, originally painted red, the old color showing beneath the later white, and is sumounted by a spire, with open belfry and a weather vane, which used to puzzle our child brains to ascertain what it was intended to represent. It has five entrances, two of which admit to the gallery. Passing in by the door, opening upon the graveyard, and near which was our family pew, we look up a broad aisle to the pulpit, which, small and closely walled in, soars aloft toward the ceiling, and is surmounted by a sounding board, like a gigantic candle extinguisher, supported by an iron rod, the possible breaking of which often aroused our infantile speculations as to what, in that event, would become of the preacher! It was reached by a lofty stairway running up in front. At right angles to our aisle runs another as broad, connecting the two other doors. Aisles run around the sides of the audience room, and the pews are so arranged that everybody seems to be facing every body else! A wide gallery extends around three sides, resounding often with the creaking of new brogans, which the black wearers were not at all disposed to suppress. The communion table and benches reach the entire length of the broad aisle to the pulpit; the whole covered with the whitest and finest of linen (our mother's special care). A cloth of the same kind conceals from view at its head the sacred symbols of our Lord's atoning death. There is above a single row of sashed windows, out of reach, and transoms over the solid shutters of the windows below; but not a sign of a stove in the church, although the air sometimes is frosty, and the shut up atmosphere occasionally of the temperature of the vaults in the cemetery hard by. And brides in the olden time, in mid-winter, came to these services clad in muslin, with only the protection of a shawl, and in paper-soled slippers, laced up the ankles. Why there never was any way of warming the church I never knew, nor heard explained. Doubtless some caught their death of the cold, which often made us children shiver and long for the benediction which would dismiss us to the sunny sides of the houses without or to their fires within. It was not, however, ordinarily bitterly cold for the winters were for the most part mild.

All things having been prepared, there is a half-hour's prayer-meeting, attended by such worshipers as have arrived early.

At eleven o'clock the regular communion service begins, with an invocation from one of the pastors; for we always had two. An earnest, well-written, often eloquent, always solemn, sermon is preached from a manuscript, either by the venerable Rev. Robert Quarterman, long since gone to his reward or his young and handsome coadjutor, Rev. I. S. K.

Axson, now living in Georgia, a feeble old man; * the long list of names of members received at a meeting of Session two weeks before, and "propounded" the Sunday preceding, is read again, and white and black candidates advance together, the last marshalled by the colored preacher, Toney Stevens, a slave. The candidates for baptism kneel and receive from the marble font, at which all, white and black, infant and adult, are baptized, the sacred sign of God's covenant love. The new members dismissed to their seats, one of the pastors gives out the hymn of institution (none other was ever sung), "'Twas on that dark, that doleful night;" during the singing of it the communicants fill the seats at the long tables and adjacent pews; the non-professors among the blacks have not been admitted to the galleries above, as there is not room. After the consecrating prayer, a tender address is made, and first the bread is distributed in the same silver baskets and at the same time, to all the communicants, white and black, below and above; another address, and the wine is passed around by the deacons, my venerated sire one of them. The number of black communicants is so large, that Toney Stevens comes down from the gallery to replenish the gold-lined silver goblets from the basket of wine in bottles near the pulpit; and as the wine is poured out, its gurgling in the solemn silence smites distinctly upon our young ears, and the whole house is filled with the aroma of the pure imported Madeira. Communicants overlooked in the distribution of the "elements" are asked to signify the fact by raising the right hand; and if any have been passed by (which never occurred), they will be waited upon. We children, awed and almost frightened spectators, look on from our pews upon the solemnities, which suggest sad thoughts of a possible separation which the judgment may, like the communion table, make between us and our beloved parents!

A prayer, doxology and benediction close the solemn and impressive service-solemn and impressive it seems to me upon the review, as nowhere else.

We refresh ourselves in the hour's intermission from the abundant "cold snacks," we called them, or lunches; sun ourselves, and walk down the road or in the graveyard. Immediately at the close of the communion service a great volume of musical sound, mellowed by the distance, comes up from the African church, in the edge of the forest, where godly Toney Stevens, the carpenter, is about to hold forth to his dusky charge. I have heard more artistic singing, but never heartier or more worshipful elsewhere.

But the bell, whose iron tongue, to our young imaginations, was endowed literally with speech, is saying, "Come along! come along!" Another sermon is preached, and horses are found harnessed and vehicles ready, and the mighty congregation disperse to their several homes. The sun is low in the western horizon when we arrive at our plantation home and sit down to a late dinner. Sunday clothes are folded up and put away, and the easier fitting every-day garments and old shoes are, to our immense relief, once more put on. A Sunday-school for the young people of the plantation, conducted in a spare room of our house by one of my sisters, in which hymns are memorized and sung, and Dr. C. C. Jones' Catechism taught, closes the public religious services of the day. After supper and prayers, tired, we all retire to our early couches; but refreshed by the rest, duties and worship of God's hallowed day, and ready on the morrow to take up with new courage and energy the tasks and burdens of secular life.

Such is a picture of a "Sacrament Sunday in old Midway," as it comes back to me, like "memories of joys that are departed, pleasant but mournful to the soul."

By such days of resting and of holy convocation were masters and servants, realizing even on earth the communion of saints, fitted for the same blessed home, in which multitudes of them have long since met, to keep an eternal celebration of their common deliverance from the bonds of sin and death and hell, and investment with the spiritual liberty wherewith Christ maketh his people free!

Blessed be the God of my fathers, that my early life was shaped by such influences! May they abide with all the sons and daughters of old Midway for ever!

CHAPTER XII.

MISSIONARY TO THE BLACKS-A SKETCH OF HIS LIFE

I RECALL now a quarrel with a sister a little older than myself, my constant playmate. It was about a fancied resemblance to a preacher. She had roached up her short-cut hair before the glass up stairs, and asserted that she looked like Dr. Jones. I, on the contrary, disputing the statement and claiming the exclusive honor of resemblance, a controversy arose, whose settlement, owing to the outcry raised, was adjourned to our mother's room. How it was finally adjusted in that child's court of final appeal is not remembered now; but the incident is quoted to show in what high esteem the children of the planter's household held one who gave his life to the evangelization of the negro.

The first distinct remembrance of him and his of me, as he told me in after years, was as follows: With that mania for destroying animal life which, at some period, seems to take possession of boys, I was engaged in the evening twilight in slaying, with a long fishing pole, the bats which, in incredible number, come out upon their nightly foraging expeditions from the crevices in the frame work of the horse gin. I heard a horse's footfalls and looked up, and the missionary to the blacks, meeting an appointment sent on to my father, rode by on his way to the quarters with a pleasant greeting and inquiry as to the nature of my employment; and without perhaps what might have been an apposite lecture upon "cruelty to animals." It was Rev. Charles Colcock Jones.

Allow a loving hand to sketch briefly the life of one of the noblest men God ever made by his creative skill and regenerating grace; and with whom, to the unspeakable profit of his piety and ministry, he was permitted, as a member of his family, to be associated in the forming period of both. I condense from a full biographical sketch prepared by myself, and published in *The Dead of the Synod of Georgia*, by Rev. Dr. J. S. Wilson, then of Atlanta, Ga.

Charles Colcock Jones, the son of Captain John Jones and Susannah Hyrn Jones, was born at Liberty Hall, his father's plantation residence, in Liberty county, Ga., December 20th, 1804, and was baptized in Midway Church by Rev. Cyrus Gildersleeve. Upon the death of his father, while he was still an infant, the sole care of him was devolved upon his mother, who, of Huguenot descent, was a woman of great excellence of character and sterling piety, and, like Hannah of old, consecrated her son to the ministry.

Again bereaved in his fifth year, he was reared by his uncle, Captain Joseph Jones, who, although not at the time a professing Christian, did by the orphan a father's part so nobly as to win his everlasting gratitude, filial affection, and obedience.

Receiving an excellent common school education at Sunbury, under a noted teacher of the day, Rev. Dr. William McWir, he, at the early age of fourteen, entered and continued in a counting-room in the city of Savannah six years-a business experience of signal service to him in after years. While thus employed, the young clerk spent his evening hours in historical studies and in the mastery of Edwards' abstruse treatise on "*The Will*." And such was his industry, system and integrity, that at the close of his novitiate he could have commanded, it was said, any position in mercantile life in that city. But it was not the Lord's will that the clerk should become the merchant. A dangerous sickness, bringing him to the verge of the grave, was the instrument in God's hands of his awakening and conversion; and at the age of seventeen he connected himself with his ancestral church at Midway, by whose pastor, Rev. Mr. Murphy, his mind was first turned toward the gospel ministry.

Owing, perhaps, to the frequent visits of the venerable Dr. Ebenezer Porter, of Andover, to his native county, he went North and entered himself as a student in the noted Phillips Academy, and subsequently in the Seminary in that place. Here, for the first time, although now twenty years old, he took in hand his Latin grammar. Three years and a half were spent in his literary and theological studies in these famous institutions. With the president, Dr. Porter, he was upon the most intimate terms; and he has been heard to say that, visiting him at all hours, there was not one in which, at some time, he had not found this godly man upon his knees.

From Andover he went to Princeton, then under Drs. Archibald Alexander and Samuel Miller, and after eighteen months' study in that noble school of the prophets, he was licensed to preach by the Presbytery of New Brunswick. In November, 1830, he was united in marriage to his cousin, Miss Mary Jones, a woman of decided piety and uncommon strength of intellect and character, who was always in fullest sympathy with him in his intellectual pursuits and his missionary labors. Preaching for a period of four or five months in his native county as opportunity offered, in 1831 he became stated supply of the First Presbyterian Church of Savannah Ga.,and was, after a short term of ministerial labor, installed pastor, the services, by request, being held in the Independent Presbyterian church, of which the noted evangelist, Dr. Daniel Baker, was then pastor. After eighteen months of conscientious and faithful service and laborious work in this, his first and only pastoral charge, he was constrained, by a sense of duty, to devote himself entirely to the great work of his life, to which his attention had been turned while a student in Princeton, and fuller preparation for which led him to accept his only pastoral charge, *viz.*, the Evangelization of the Negro.

The same motive, as I know, led him twice to accept a call to the chair of Church History in Columbia Seminary, and the important position of Secretary of the Board of Domestic Missions of the *ante bellum* Presbyterian Church.

With the interruptions above mentioned, in which he kept the ruling passion of his life steadily in view, he devoted his entire energies of body and mind, for a term of five years, to uninterrupted, direct, personal labor, such as few men could or would have stood, among the blacks of his native county, at his own charges, and with wonderful success. The seeds of the disease which finally terminated his earthly career were probably laid in his system while laboring night and day in the malarial regions of Liberty county, the destructive effect of which it needed only the confinement of office work in Philadelphia, and pressure of responsibility and of wearing toil (for he was a man who put his whole soul into whatever he undertook) to complete. Reluctantly resigning his position, he came home to rest and recuperate. The hope of ultimate recovery was not, however, destined to be realized. And here begins the invalid life of this man of God, protracted through ten years, in which gradually declining from what is known as wasting palsy-a rare disease-but with intellect undimmed, he did more work with pen and tongue than many a minister in full possession of health and vigor. He preached constantly, sitting, when unable to stand, upon a chair and a platform which he had had constructed and placed in the African church at Midway. Often did I hear my parents remark of him and his preaching at this time: "Dr. Jones is not far from heaven." It is a singular fact that this incessant worker, from an injury received in childhood, lived and labored with only one lung in active play, occasioning often a sense of weariness in the vocal organs unknown to one in perfect health.

The death of this good and great man, of whose labors we shall speak more particularly at another time, and which occurred when he was only fifty nine, formed a fitting close to his life.

No one watched the symptoms of approaching dissolution with greater care and composure than himself. His son, Dr. Joseph Jones, now of New Orleans, had, and still probably has, a minute history of the entire progress of his disease, written out by himself, and continued up to the last month of his life. A period of unusual mortality among his servants, and solicitude on their account, and his anxiety about the war, it is believed, hastened his end. Not many months before his death he remarked to his eldest son, Charles C. Jones, LL. D. now of Augusta, Ga.: "My son, I am living in momentary expectation of death, but the thought of its approach causes me no alarm. The frail tabernacle must soon be taken down. I only wait God's time." Four days before his departure he makes this record in his journal:

"*March* 12, 1863.-Have been very weak and declining since renewal of the cold on the 1st instant in the church (Midway). My disease appears to be drawing to a conclusion. May the Lord make me to say in that hour, in saving faith and love, 'Into thy hands I commit my spirit; Thou hast redeemed me, O Lord God of truth.' (Ps. xxxi. 5.) So has our blessed Saviour taught us by His own example to do, and blessed are they who die in the Lord."

On the morning of the 16th, on which he died, having bathed and dressed himself, as was his wont, with scrupulous care, he breakfasted down stairs with the family, and then spent the forenoon in his steady up stairs, sometimes sitting up and some times reclining, conversing with his wife and sister, but with difficulty, and suffering from restlessness and debility. Some of the sweet promises of Christ's presence with His people in their passage through the dark valley being repeated to him by his companion, he sweetly replied: "In health we repeat these promises, but now they are realities." She again remarking, "I feel assured that the Saviour is with you," he answered: "I am nothing but a poor sinner; I renounce myself and all self-justification, trusting only in the free, unmerited righteousness of the Lord Jesus Christ." To his sons, absent in the army, he sent this message: "Tell them both to lead lives of godly men in Christ Jesus, in uprightness and integrity." Upon the suggestion of his wife that he should retire to his room and rest awhile, he arose, and, supported on either hand by her and a loved sister, he walked into the adjoining chamber, playfully remarking, "How honored I am in being waited upon by two ladies!" Reclining upon his bed, in a few moments, without a struggle, a sigh, a gasp, he gently fell asleep in Jesus. A glory almost unearthly, and which awed the very servants, rested after death upon his noble countenance. Shortly afterwards, just as he was, in the same garments he had put on in the morning, with his white cravat unsoiled, and with every fold as his own hands had arranged it, he was borne back to his study, where, surrounded by the authors he had so loved in life, he seemed to rest in a peaceful sleep, until the third day following, when, after appropriate services, conducted by the Rev. Dr. D. L. Buttolph, in Midway meeting-house, his mortal remains were committed to the grave, in the venerable cemetery where his own parents and many generations of God's saints are awaiting the resurrection morn.

CHAPTER XIII.

A MISSIONARY TO THE BLACKS-HIS LABORS AMONG THEM.

DR. JONES' work among the slaves may be divided into his labors among them, and his labors for them; it is proposed in this letter to sketch the first.

The main field of his missionary work was what was known as "the Fifteenth Company District of Liberty county, Ga." According to the census of 1830, just three years before his first report of his labors to "The Association for the Religious Instruction of the Negroes," the whole population of the county was as follows: Whites, 1,544; blacks, 5,729; of these, owing to the lands being suitable to the production of rice and Sea Island cotton, 4,540 were concentrated in the district just named.

Here for five consecutive years of literally uninterrupted activity, this devoted servant of God, by day and by night, in summer's heat and winter's cold, in sunshine and storm, and at his own charges labored for the salvation and consequent elevation of the race to whose good he had consecrated his splendid talents-gifts which, as they at intervals called him to the highest positions in the church, would have fitted him for the most important pastoral charge in the land.

He had six preaching stations, in which there was either a house of worship, gladly tendered by the whites, or a building put up, at his suggestion, by the masters for the exclusive use of their people. These were located in the most thickly settled neighborhoods, and accessible not only to pedestrians, but to the children whom, with the adults, he gathered into his Sunday schools. Besides these regular

Sabbath appointments, he held meetings during the week upon the plantations, where the feeble could be supplied with the word of life, and he could perform pastoral work to those who were too aged even to attend the neighborhood church.

I give from memory a sketch of a Sabbath's labors. The missionary has come from his distant plantation home, necessitating an early start. As soon as possible, a prayer-meeting is held, at which competent "watchmen" lead in prayer. Next follows the sermon and its accompanying services of song and prayer. In the afternoon there is the Sunday-school for both adults and children, in which all are orally taught Scripture truth and doctrine, drilled thoroughly in the use of Jones' Catechism, and all interspersed with hymns and tunes learned, the one leader doing all that is done in an ordinary school by superintendent and teachers together. Then follows an inquiry-meeting for the serious and candidates for membership. Then a meeting of the "watchmen" of the district is held, in which the pastor receives detailed reports of the state of religion and conduct of the members on the various plantations, and disciplines delinquents when necessary. And all this is interspersed with wise counsels given to these humble under-shepherds appointed by church and pastor as his helpers. The sun is low in the sky when the servant of God, weary yet rejoicing, turns his steps homeward.

The week, spent largely in his study (for he prepared thoroughly for his services), and in the oversight of his plantations, does not witness rest from his preaching labors; for he has appointments during the week upon all the plantations open to him, as all were in course of time, and as his strength permits.

His custom was to send on, some time in advance to a planter favoring his work, an appointment for an evening in the week; leaving to him all the details of arrangement. Sometimes the service was held in the planter's mansion, the people bringing with them their own benches or chairs, and sometimes in one of the negro houses, or the "praise house," built for the purpose. On his own plantation it was a neat plastered building, with belfry and bell. If in the planter's house, the parlor was illuminated by candles and a cheerful fire on the hearth. If in the quarters, often the main illumination would come from the great wide chimney with its roaring fire, no matter how warm the night chanced to be, with a single candle for the preacher. Here this devoted servant of God faithfully preached, and used "great plainness of speech." I have myself been amazed, as I listened, to see how, without the loss of a particle of that dignity which was at once characteristic of the man, and of his conceptions of the sacred ministry, he came down completely to the level of the intellectual calibre of his humble hearers. The night service was followed or preceded by visits to the aged and sick. Not a few of these services were held, with the temperature without almost that of summer, in small rooms, crammed with workers in their work-a-day clothes, with no window to open because of draft, and a hot fire on the hearth. This experience, as I have heard him say, was trying in no ordinary degree to him; for he was a polished gentleman, and neat in person and habits beyond most even of his own race.

We need not wonder at the gradual subsidence of the suspicion, distrust and opposition encountered at the outset, on the part of some ungodly planters, when we peruse the wise rules adopted by him, mark his fidelity in preaching the whole counsel of God, and read the account of some of the precious fruits of his apostolical labors. With these we close. In his tenth report, in which he "reviews the work from the commencement," he writes: "I laid down the following rules of action, which I have ever endeavored to observe faithfully:

"1. To visit no plantation without permission, and, when permitted, never without previous notice.

"2. To have nothing to do with the civil condition of the negroes, or with their plantation affairs

"3. To hear no tales respecting their owners, or drivers, or work, and to keep within my own breast whatever of a private nature might incidentally come to my knowledge.

"4. To be no party to their quarrels, and have no quarrels with them, but cultivate justice, impartiality, and universal kindness.

"5. To condemn, without reservation, every vice and evil among them, in the terms of God's holy word, and to inculcate the fulfilment of every duty, whatever might be the real or apparent hazard of popularity or success.

"6. To preserve the most perfect order at all our public and private meetings.

"7. To impress the people with the great value of the privilege enjoyed of religious instruction; to invite their co-operation and throw myself upon their confidence and support.

"8. To make no attempt to create temporary excitements, or to introduce any new plans or measures; but make diligent and prayerful use of the ordinary and established means of God's appointment.

"9. To support, in the fullest manner, the peace and order of society, and to hold up to their respect and obedience all those whom God, in his providence, has placed in authority over them.

"10. To notice no slights or unkindnesses shown to me personally; to dispute with no man about the work, but depend upon the power of the truth and upon the Spirit and blessing of God, with long suffering, patience, and perseverance, to overcome opposition and remove prejudices, and ultimately bring all things right."

There is an amusing instance related by himself in his third report, and the particulars of which I heard from his own lips, illustrative of the temporary unpopularity which he drew upon himself by simply preaching the truth. "Of your missionary some have said, 'We will not hear him; he preaches to please the masters.' And once upon a time, while enforcing a certain duty" (it was the duty of not running away, and from Paul's treatment of Onesimus, whom he sent back to his master), "when enforcing a certain duty from the Scriptures which servants owe to their masters, more than one-half of my large congregation rose up and went away, every man to his house, and the part that remained seemed to remain more from personal respect to the preacher than from any liking to the doctrine."

But if he fearlessly "declared the whole counsel of God" to the slave, he no less fearlessly declared it to the master, urging, and not without success, reforms in their treatment of their servants, both as bearing upon their physical comfort and the salvation of their souls.

The natural result of his prudence and fidelity to his mission, as an expounder of God's word, was the ultimate and complete removal of the suspicion and prejudice which he at first encountered, and a boundless popularity among the colored people, such as no man ever before or since has enjoyed.

As the result of these faithful labors, the physical and moral conditions of the slaves were manifestly improved, a sense of responsibility in regard to their immortal interests awakened in the county, souls in large numbers were converted under his ministry, and saints built up and fitted for heaven. The particular record of his pastoral experience was unfortunately consumed in the fire which destroyed his residence when a Professor in the Seminary in Columbia.

One precious revival occurred during his ministry, of which there is an interesting account in his fifth report. As a result, more than a hundred members from this race were added to old Midway church in a little over a year.

The eighth annual report closes with an account of a "*protracted meeting for the negroes*," which furnishes suggestive reading to those who believe slavery was "he sum of villainies!" We quote:

"In the month of November a protracted meeting was held at Midway church in connection with the meeting of the Presbytery of Georgia, which continued a week. By universal consent of the church and congregation, *Friday and Saturday were given to the negroes for religious worship, and some who were not members, either of the church or congregation gave their people the two days. Planters who were not members of the church united cordially in it.*" (Italics mine) Services were held on Friday and Saturday twice a day for the negroes in their own church. The house could not contain the people; more without than within. On Sabbath they attended from all parts of the county. The gallery of the white church was filled, and perhaps as many remained around the doors and windows of the churches as had been accommodated with seats within. The greatest order and propriety prevailed. The members of the church were particularly grateful for the privileges allowed them, and all seemed anxious to hear the gospel. This protracted meeting for the negroes deserves to be mentioned, as an index of the interest of owners in their eternal welfare, of their willingness to grant them every opportunity of salvation, and to share the gospel with them, and of their general order, sobriety and propriety of conduct. The moral effect upon the negroes has been of the most satisfactory kind. It has given them increased respect for and attachment to their owners, and impressed them with the sincerity of their desires for their best good, and it has led them to believe more in the value and necessity of religion."

CHAPTER XIV.

A MISSIONARY TO THE BLACKS-HIS LABORS FOR THEM.

DR. C. C. JONES was, in the fullest sense of the term, a philanthropist. While his direct object was the salvation of the soul, the body was not neglected. Not content with conversion, he aimed to build up Christian character, and in every possible way he sought to awaken, and not without marvellous success, the entire South to a deeper sense of responsibility for the temporal and spiritual welfare of the slave.

I. *His labors for their physical improvement.*In his reports to "The Association for the Religious Instruction of the Negroes," and in his paper read before Synod, he fearlessly pressed upon his fellow slave-holders their duties to the bodies of their slaves. In his second report, in 1834, he uses this language, which may sound strangely to some ears: "While we think that we see an improvement in their physical condition upon past years, we would say that there is still vast room for improvement. *They are entitled to a far larger portion of the avails of their labor than they have hitherto been accustomed to receive.*" (Italics mine.) In his third report, in 1835, he uses this strong language, addressed to his fellow-citizens and fellow-Christians: "If you do not labor and be at some sacrifice to improve their *physical condition*, providing more liberally, and to the extent of your means, for their comfort, in good houses, good clothing, and good food; if you do not regulate their *discipline* so as to maintain authority without injustice, they cannot and will not, value your instruction." In an elaborate report of a committee appointed by the Synod of South Carolina and Georgia in

1833, endorsed, "Prepared by C. C. J.," and having for its chairman Moses Waddel, D. D., and such additional names as B. M. Palmer, D. D., S. S. Davis, S. J. Cassels, James English, etc., which was adopted and published to the world, the following bold language is found: "The principle which regulates duty in slavery on the part of the master has been thus defined: 'Get all you can, and give back as little as you can'; and on the part of the servants the reverse, 'Give as little as you can, and get back all you can.' When we remember what human nature is, and when we observe the conduct of masters and servants, we fear that there is too much truth as to the existence of this principle." "Religion will tell the master that his servants are his fellow-creatures, and that he has a Master in heaven to whom he shall account for his treatment of them. The master will be led to inquiries of this sort: In what kind of houses do I permit them to live? What clothes do I give them to wear? What food to eat, what privileges to enjoy? In what temper and manner and proportion to their crimes are they punished?" Extracts might also be given in which he urges the provision of sufficient house-room for growing families, to secure privacy, and exhorts masters to prevent, by authority, open immorality in the slaves, and to abstain from all violation of the marriage bond by separating husband and wife.

Now, it required uncommon boldness to speak and write thus, when the insidious efforts of abolitionists to stir up the slaves to the use of torch and knife had rendered the Southern mind exceedingly sensitive and suspicious; traces of which sentiments are to be found in references in some of his earlier reports.

In his tenth report (1845), in which he reviews ten years of work among masters and servants, he gratefully notes improvement in these words: "The religious instruction of the negroes has had *a good effect upon masters*. We observe a milder discipline and kinder feelings and greater attention to the morals and comforts of the people, and, as a consequence, *their physical condition is improved*." In his twelfth report, presented in 1847, he remarks: "Greater attention is paid to their clothing, their food, their houses, their comforts, their family relations and morality at home. And the appearance of the people, both at home and abroad, indicates this increased care and attention on the part of their owners."

II. *Their spiritual improvement*. His work was not done when the slave became, through grace, Christ's freeman; he proceeded to build him up into a citizen of Zion. And recognizing the agency of divine truth in this process, he not only earnestly preached but, diligently taught young and old, in the only way then possible, that is, *orally*.

Reminding the uninformed reader that abolitionists of that day did not scruple to publish and mail the most incendiary documents, and even to place them in the very packages used in the Southern kitchens, he will understand the motive of some laws passed in the South, forbidding the instruction of the negro in the art of reading. It was our mistake; but there was in the fact just stated at least a palliation, and in most States the law was a dead letter. The white children were always ready to, and did, teach any who wished it, to read. We quote from the Synodical report this faithful statement of this difficulty in evangelizing the negro: "It is universally the fact throughout the slave-holding States, that either custom or law prohibits to them the acquisition of letters, and consequently they can have no access to the Scriptures. The proportion that read is infinitely small; the Bible, so far as they can read it themselves, is to all intents and purposes a sealed book, so that they are dependent for their knowledge of Christianity upon oral instruction, as much so as the unlettered heathen, when first visited by our missionaries. If our laws in their operation seal up the Scriptures to the negroes, we should not allow them to suffer in the least degree, so far as any effort on our part may be necessary, for want of knowledge of their contents."

Compelled thus to rely upon oral instruction for the communication, not only of saving truth to children, but more advanced religious knowledge to adults, he was very early in his work among the slaves constrained to prepare a manual of his own. We find an allusion to it in his first report to "the Association." "The children and youth have been to all appearance much interested. I instruct them from a catechism which I am attempting to prepare for them." In the tenth report he gives this interesting account of the causes which led to the composition of this interesting manual: "A difficulty presented itself at the very beginning of my Sabbath-school instruction. There were no *books*! I tried all the catechisms. Necessity forced me to attempt something myself. I prepared the lessons weekly, and tried them and corrected them from the schools, and the result was; "*The Catechism of Scripture Doctrine and Practice*;" or, to give the title more fully, "A Catechism of Scripture Doctrine and Practice, for Families and Sabbath-schools.

Designed also for the oral instruction of colored persons. By Charles C. Jones."

He steadily refused the request of the Presbyterian Board of Publication to publish an edition with the reference to the negro left off, for use in white schools. His method of composing it, as I learned from his own lips, was to ask the question and then note the answer, and frequently the extemporaneous reply of the negro pupil would be so superior in plainness to his written answer, that he would substitute it for his own. This catechism was translated into Armenian by Rev. Dr. J. B. Adger when a missionary in Syria, and by Rev. John Quarterman into one of the dialects of China, and used in both countries. It was universally adopted in Liberty county and in many parts of the South, and found invaluable in the family as well as in the instruction of the slaves. The writer used it to great advantage in his own household in the religious training of his children, and in preparing colored catechumens for church membership. Here is what its author has to say of the possibility of communicating truth orally to the slave: "That they are apt in receiving instruction, none have ever doubted who have favored us with their presence for a single Sabbath. No difference will be perceived generally between them and other children in like circumstances. There are scholars who can repeat thirty pages of the catechism with accuracy, and by varying the form of the questions, and so putting their knowledge to proof, it will be seen that they recite with *intelligence* also. To those who are ignorant of letters, *their memory is their book*. That faculty is capable of astonishing improvement. Knowledge may be communicated and retained to almost any extent through oral instruction alone. In a recent examination of one of the schools, I was forcibly struck with their remembrance of passages of Scripture. Those questions which turned upon and called for passages of *Scripture*, the scholars answered more readily than any other. It was with them as with all youth, a Scripture fact, a Scripture story, once told and impressed, is stamped on the tablet of memory forever."

We venture the assertion that the slave population of Liberty county, enjoying these advantages, had a clearer and more systematic and thorough knowledge of Scripture history, doctrine and practice than many a white community this day who can read and have only such preaching as can be supplied by some Evangelical denominations. I know from experience that the faithful instruction enjoyed in that favored county through the apostolical labors of this godly minister woke up the mind of the African to the agitation of questions which astonished me. For example, an intelligent carpenter, upon whom it was my custom to call to lead in prayer, once took me aside before service and asked me how he should represent to himself the three persons of the God-head in prayer so as to avoid idolatry!

Under this combined instruction of the pulpit and Sabbath-school, multitudes of precious souls were not only converted, but trained for earth and heaven.

It were to be wished that some liberal-hearted Christian could be induced to furnish the means to publish an edition of this most valuable Catechism, with only such few changes as would be necessary in their altered circumstances, for the use of our colored population. Prepared by one who loved, gave his life to, and studied and *knew the race more perfectly than any man living or dead*, the Catechism would, I doubt not, be as useful now as it was in the past.

NOTE.-A copy of the Catechism in my library fell, with the rest of my books, into the hands of Sherman's soldiers. Strange to say, the chapter on the duties of masters and servants is undisturbed, but the chapter on "What the Church of God is," has suffered, both from the knife and the pencil of a zealous Baptist, presumably a chaplain, an enemy to infant baptism.

CHAPTER XV.

A MISSIONARY TO THE BLACKS-HIS LABORS FOR THEM.

IT was impossible in the last chapter to present, without engrossing too much space, even a sketch of Dr. Jones' labors for the slave. Three things remain to be signalized under this head.

III. *His agency in the formation of an Association in his native county for the furtherance of this cause.*

I have in my library a bound volume of pamphlets, once the property of Dr. Jones, and now mine by inheritance through his daughter. It is to me a precious and invaluable treasure. It contains the report of the Committee on the Religious Instruction of the Colored Population, adopted by the then undivided Synod of South Carolina and Georgia, December, 1833, of which, as shown by his penciled endorsement, he, although not the chairman, was the author; thirteen Annual Reports of C. C. Jones to "The Association for the Religious Instruction of the Negroes," extending from 1833 to 1848; proceedings of a meeting held in Charleston by the friends of the cause in 1845, with a report of a committee and an address to the holders of slaves in South Carolina, the result of that assembly of Christians and patriots of different denominations, and in which figure such noted South Carolina names as Huger, Capers, Cotesworth Pinckney, Barnwell, Rhett, Alston, Grimes, Memminger, Ravennel, and other names as prominent in the church as Dr. McWhir, Rev. Mr. Barnwell, Dr. C. C. Jones, Dr. Thomas Smyth, Dr. Benjamin Gildersleeve, Thomas S. Clay, etc.; and also Dr. Jones' suggestions on the religious instruction of the negroes in the Southern States. A penciled note in Dr. Jones' hand-writing, at the bottom of the first page of the second report, states, "the first report was not to be had, as copies were burnt up," (in the burning of his residence in Columbia). Either he or his companion afterwards recovered it from some owner, and pinned it, with its leaves uncut, in its proper place. It seems providential that these reports should have been all preserved; for as will be seen farther on, they contain an account, not simply of what one man and one county did, but what Southern Christians of every denomination had been doing for years for the salvation of their slaves.

In the tenth report we have this account of the origin of an association of which Dr. Jones was the founder, and whose influence extended far beyond the bounds of the favored county which was for many years its home:

"The spiritual wants and condition of the negroes in the county, their ignorance of the gospel, and the duty and the best means of affording them suitable and systematic instruction, were subjects of conversation with the ministers and certain members of the churches for some time in the winter of 1831; and on the 10th of March a meeting of persons favorable to the adoption of some efficient plan for their religious instruction was called in Riceboro'. Upon consultation, it was determined to form an *Association* for the purpose, and a committee was appointed to prepare a report and a constitution, and Rev. C. C. Jones to deliver an address at another meeting, to be held in the same place on the 28th of March. At that meeting the address was delivered, the constitution reported and adopted, and the present Association formed. *Twenty-nine* individuals, in the course of some weeks, signed the constitution."

From the constitution, published in the seventh report, we emphasize only the following particulars as bearing upon our object in these letters. Officered as usual, any one might become a member by signing the constitution and paying an annual subscription of two dollars. To an executive committee was entrusted the entire supervision of the work of colored evangelization, in the selection of stations and appointment of "teacher or teachers"-that is, laborers. Meeting annually, a report or address was to be made by some person appointed by the Association.

Article VI. reads: "The instructions of this Association shall be altogether oral, embracing the general principles of the Christian religion, as understood by orthodox Christians, avoiding, in the public instruction of the negroes, doctrines which particularly distinguish the different denominations of the country from each other."

Designedly undenominational, its first officers were: President, Rev. Robert Quarterman (Presbyterian); Vice-President, Rev. Samuel S. Law (Baptist). Executive Committee: Thomas Bacon (Baptist), Thomas Mallard (Presbyterian), etc.; and Missionary, Rev. Charles C. Jones (Presbyterian).

From the first, composed of the best and most prominent citizens of the county, this noble Association, by its annual meetings, to which the public was invited; by the information collected and published, by its indefatigable missionary, concerning the needs of the negro, and what was being done, not only in the county, but throughout the South; and by the stirring addresses delivered from time to time by himself and other ministers, communicated a constant impulse to the work at home. As will be seen, it was no small instrument of stimulating Christians throughout the South to similar activity.

IV. *His personal efforts outside the county and State to interest the church and country in the cause.*

n the interval between his two periods of work among the slaves of Liberty county, he made an extensive tour through the States, and wherever he journeyed he embraced every opportunity in interesting his fellow-citizens in the evangelization of the negro. I extract from the fifth report.

Referring to "an extended and protracted journey through the Northern and Middle States," he remarks: "There was no subject more solicitously inquired into by judicious and pious men with whom we met; and frequent opportunities were afforded me by special invitation, of the most respectable kind, for laying before the people assembled for the purpose, a sketch of what was doing in the Southern States for the instruction of the negroes in the principles of Christianity, and of expressing the views and feelings of the Southern churches on the subject. These addresses were received with unanimous satisfaction, saving one unimportant exception."

As a Professor of Church History in Columbia, he not only, if I remember, organized a flourishing colored Sunday.school, but embraced the many opportunities, public and private, which constantly occurred in his intimate associations with the students to turn their minds toward the neglected colored population of the South. And the engrossing cares of his official life as Secretary of Home Missions did not induce forgetfulness of the negro; for he sought to shape the work of that important arm of the church with decided and special reference to that portion of the home field found on the plantations of the South.

V. *His labor for them in his correspondence and publications.*

The annual reports give evidence of a vast personal correspondence with men all over the South upon the subject of the negro a correspondence, with perhaps some assistance from members of his family, conducted mainly by his own pen.

His reports and addresses, prepared for and delivered before ecclesiastical bodies, master-pieces in their way, were published under their official sanction, and widely circulated throughout the South, stirring the churches of every name as with the blast of a trumpet.

His annual reports to the local Association, as they were intended for a larger audience, so through the press were they distributed throughout the South, and had a wonderful effect in arousing the Southern conscience in regard to their duty to the slave. In the second report I find this allusion to this method of promoting the cause: "It may be gratifying to the Association to know that two editions of their report for the past year have been printed, and there is now a demand for a *third*." An extract from one of the many letters received pays this tribute to his work: "Your noiseless labors in Liberty county are not unobserved by the Christian world, and are watched with intense interest by many."

While we would not discount the labors of countless conscientious masters and mistresses in instructing and catechising their slaves, and of faithful ministers who labored among them, and prominent Christians who with tongue and pen wrought for the salvation of the slave, with a fidelity which doubtless will receive recognition "at that day," we do not hesitate to say that Charles *Colcock* Jones, whether his labors among or his labors for them with tongue and pen be considered, deserves more than any man who has ever lived the title of "The Apostle to the Negro Slave!"

This *résumé* of his labors for the redemption of the negro cannot be more appropriately closed than in these words, which disclose the great loving heart of this eminent servant of Christ:

"I cannot describe the peculiar and joyful feelings that have possessed my mind when I have seen penitents from this long neglected and degraded people inquiring what they must do to be saved. It is not building upon another man's foundation. You are in the highways and hedges. You gather the first fruits yourself, and the undivided joy takes full possession of the soul."

CHAPTER XVI.

RELIGIOUS ANECDOTES OF THE NEGRO.

I AM quite sure that our readers will be glad to have the following anecdotes, illustrative of negro character, and of the results of the faithful instructions of Rev. Charles Colcock Jones and his fellow laborers, the planters of Liberty county, Ga. I will not occupy space with comments.

Under the head of "Degree of Religious Intelligence Among the People," he gives the following incidents:

Said one, speaking of the religious advantages enjoyed: "Sir, the people never had the gospel so opened to their understandings before, many walked in darkness for the want of the true Light; but all the power of God is needed to make them profit by it; God only can open men's hearts." Another: "If any are lost in this Liberty county, it will be their fault. They have light enough, and close at hand, and privileges enough to go to. Yea, more, the light is brought on the plantations and set down at their very doors."

An observing man gave it as his opinion "that the people were better able now to understand the gospel from ministers *preaching to the whites*than formerly. For example, they were able to follow the ministers with their copy; whereas, beforetime, they could not do so at all. The reason he believed to be an increase of knowledge *through the Sabbath-schools* and*direct preaching to the negroes.* He thought ministers did much better in preaching when they put down their copy."

The following is a dialogue between a man and a woman: "I saw you talking to the minister before meeting, and you told him everything that was doing on the plantation." "Good woman, I did not" "Sir, you did. How came the minister to know what was done on the place only *Saturday night?* Everybody in the church knew who he was talking about. Do you think people like to be carried into the pulpit and turned every which way for people to look at?" "Woman, you wrong me; you have not the right understanding of the matter. Does not God know *all* things?" "Well, sir, I

know that as well as you do!""But, woman, put your knowledge to use. Does not the minister preach the *Word of God?*Does not the word of God know all things? Was it not made to suit everybody? Well, then, the minister did not know in himself anything about you, *but the word of God did*; and by the way you speak now, it *fit* you exactly; and so it proves itself to you to be the Word of God that knoweth all things, and, instead of being *vexed* with the word of God, you had better *straighten* your ways and be at peace with it."

A member of the church gave the preacher the following encouragement; "You preach Sunday; you preach in the week; many hear. The seed falls on *much* ground; now some will turn and come; the good seed will sometimes fall on good ground; so keep on preaching; keep throwing your net, you will catch some."

During a revival a "watchman" insisted: "Sir, do not take the people *in too soon; instruct them well;* make them wait; such and such men were taken into the church during the revival in Mr.-'s time; they partook of the sacrament once or twice, and there ended their religion. It *is easy taking in, but it is hard putting out."*

Mounting his horse at a close of a plantation meeting, the preacher was thus addressed: "Sir, please to come as often as you can. Plantation meetings do as much good as *Sunday* meetings; because on Sunday many *garnish* themselves and go to church for show; they hear, but do not attend. On the plantation *they do not garnish themselves*, nor look around, but give attention to the Word."

One member asked counsel of another: "Is twice a week often enough to hold plantation prayers?" It was answered: "No! my brother. Do we eat and drink every day? Does God keep the people on the plantation from evil every day? Does he keep them from evil every night? Must we not thank God for these mercies? We cannot give God thanks enough for it if we try. Do we not *sin* every day, and every day need God's pardon and God's help to do our duty? My brother, *we must pray every day for ourselves, and hold plantation prayers every night.*"

A "watchman" who was giving instruction to a house servant, for some reason not very creditable to himself, did not wish the fact known to the mistress, and told the woman not to tell to whom she had been. Another watchman reproved him thus: "You do wrong. You are leading the woman to God *by the way of the devil.* While you tell her to be *honest and sincere before God*, you teach her to *lie to men..*"

At an inquiry meeting one answered: "I came to church here; I went home and thought of the sermon; my sins troubled me; I went to my mistress; she told me to go, pray and confess my sins to God, and beg him to forgive me and give me a new heart for Christ's sake." Another said: "My master spoke to me about my soul, and I considered what he said, and my sins troubled me." Another: "I was in the prayer-house on the plantation; I was careless. At the close I was weak as water. I was afraid I should die and be lost; I felt very wicked; I felt I needed assistance. I could not save myself." Another: "I felt *very mean* on account of my sin; I felt I needed a Saviour. That feeling made me go to Christ." Said another: "Ah! sir; my heart and the Bible are *not one.*"

The experience of a young man believed to be converted was thus related by himself: "Religion began in me by little and little, and deepened as I went forward. A full year or more before I hoped I was converted, I ofttimes would go out of the house from among my wicked companions, leave music and dancing, and go aside and pray, and come back; but was ashamed to tell that I had gone out to pray." His attention was particularly called to religion by what he had read in *Webster's Spelling Book*! Wishing to learn to read, he got a book and spelled out: "*Sin will lead us to pain and woe;*" *and again*: "*A bad man can take no rest day or night;*" and he felt that it was so-he could rest neither day or night. He went on until it was impossible to contain his feelings, and then made them known.

This young man also related a conversation with one of his old dissipated companions: "You and I can never be as great (intimate) as we have been, because I do not love your ways *now* as I *used* to do, neither do you love my ways. To be as great as we have been, *you must come to me*, or I must *go back to you*. Go back to you I cannot; *you must come to me*. Nor can I *be with you* as before. A doctor visits a sick man and gives him medicine, and goes away. Now suppose that doctor lives, eats and sleeps in the bed continually with the sick man, will he not be sure to catch his sickness or something from him? So if I come and eat and sleep with you, I shall be presently as bad as you are. All I can do is, come and tell you the Word, and give you instruction, according to my weak understanding, and go away; and yet I am your friend, and a better and safer friend than ever." His friend answered: "I cannot go your way." "Stop!" said he. "If I tell you where you may go and do a piece of work and get money, will you not go? Now religion is better than silver or gold; if I tell you the way you can go and seek religion, will you not go for it? You are seeking to get up a great character with master, driver, people, everybody. What will hurt your character you care for; what will not hurt your character you do not care for. After you get this character you are satisfied. You are wrong. Let me tell you, the *sinner has the meanest character* on the face of the earth. The sinner does not know it, and cannot see it, until he is brought out of it. Then he can see and know it. I know it because I see it, but you do not. I call the sinner *devil*; now this hurts your feelings. Now listen to me. *Angels* in heaven are *righteous*; *Jesus is holy*; *God* is holy; *sin is filthy*. You are a sinner; you are filthy; you are the devil! What meaner character can a man be, than be as the devil?"

The interest often felt in the conversion of their masters is strong and lively. "You know my master. It is in his power to forbid all prayer and praise on the place; *to stop the voice*. But it is not in the power of man to *destroy love in the heart*; to make us hate the God we love. *We can love in silence*. But *my master stops no man in religion*. He says he will stand in no man's way. We ring our bell and hold our prayers continually. I only wish he were a Christian. But I live in hope. I think I see an alteration. When he speaks now of the business or the plantation he says, '*If we live*,' '*If Providence permits*,' we will do this and that; in times past, he did not use to speak so."

But we must close, and we do it with two anecdotes, which bring before us our "missionary to the blacks" in the sweetness of his humility, and tenderness of his loving appreciation of the piety and fidelity of his humble co-workers in the building up of Christ's kingdom among the lowly. "There never has been an instance of an individual's declining to pray when called upon to do so. (My own experience.) Many of their prayers, though uttered in broken language, have been of great fervency, compass and expression. I can never forget the prayers of *Dembo*, a native African, for many years a member of Midway church. There was a depth of humility, a conviction of sinfulness and inability to all good, an assurance of faith, a sense of the divine presence, a nearness of access to God, a spiritual perception of, and a union with Christ as the life and righteousness of the soul, a flowing out of love, a being swallowed up in God, which I never heard before or since; and often when he closed his prayers, I felt I was as weak as water, and that I ought not to open my mouth in public, and indeed knew not what it was to pray. This modest, exemplary and holy man died full of years, in firm hope of a blessed immortality, leaving behind him the fragrance of his virtues and a bright example in all the relations of life." And *this* from one, who most of all men I have ever heard pray, lifted the suppliant into the very presence chamber of the great King, and prostrated the soul before the majesty of heaven in reverential and adoring love!

He writes: "On the death of Jack Salters, which occurred when Mr. Gildersleeve was pastor of Midway church, he was succeeded by *Sharper*, belonging to Mrs. Quarterman, a man of most remarkable integrity, piety, zeal and energy of character; who enjoyed the confidence of the entire community until his death, which occurred in the spring of 1833. He not only preached at 'the Stand,' at Midway, on the Sabbath, as his predecessors had done, but he labored with apostolical zeal more abundantly than they all. He attended regularly meetings not only at the estate of Lamberts (the plantation left by Mr. Lambert for charitable and religious purposes), and at Mr. James' plantation, but many others. His evening meetings with the people were very numerous, his influence great and solely for God. He was a special instrument in the hands of God for the moral improvement and salvation of the negroes of the county. The effects of his labors are seen on every hand at this day. He died full of years, universally lamented. I attended his funeral. It was on the green in front of Midway church, by the light of the moon. Between two and three hundred negroes were present. At the close of the services we opened the coffin. The moon shone upon his face. The people gazed upon it and lifted up their voices and wept. His sons bore him to his grave. In silence we returned to our homes, oppressed with grief at this heavy affliction of God!"

CHAPTER XVII.
WHAT WAS DONE FOR THE NEGRO BY OTHER MEN AND WOMEN, MINISTERS CHURCHES, ANDCOMMUNITIES.

ONE can but be amused with the simplicity with which George Muller avows that his great orphanage, with its two thousand inmates, was conducted entirely upon the principle of making its wants known exclusively to God. The condensed history of the straits to which it was from time to time reduced, and wonderfully relieved in answer to prayer, with the story of the governing principle and the wants of the orphans, annually published and paraded throughout the United Kingdom, was the strongest and most effective appeal for human help; his practice was more scriptural than his theory.

There was no such incompatibility between the theory and the practice of our philanthropist missionary; he combined work with prayer, and gave due credit to each.

Referring to his early commercial life, I remember to have heard him say that there was room even in a merchant's avocation for the largest exercise of intellect. Had he been permitted to serve God and his generation in that calling, he would have been among the foremost, not only in success, but intelligence; he would have familiarized himself with the history of ancient and modern commerce, with countries and their productions, with the highways of the seas and lands and modes of transportation, and the laws of finance. Now, all this thoroughness of information, breadth of view, firmness of grasp, clearness of vision, and painstaking industry, he carried into his lifework. He informed himself concerning the history of African slavery, and the numbers and condition, physical and spiritual, of the negro race in America. And bearing upon his great heart the immortal interests, not only of the four thousand slaves, constituting, we may say, his immediate pastoral charge, but of the two millions of them scattered throughout the South, he, while diligently cultivating his own particular field, took within his sympathetic vision the entire area of slavery, and labored as earnestly to have accomplished by other hands the same work he, with his co-laborers, was doing in his native county. It is this last peculiarity which makes the work I have undertaken in this letter easy. Only four out of the thirteen reports rendered to "The Association for the Religious Instruction of the Negro" are confined to county work; the balance give each, in turn, a more or less complete review of the work being done by other hands throughout the Southern church.

To relate all that was accomplished by Southern Christians and philanthropists for the salvation and elevation of the negro slave would necessitate a protracted and difficult investigation, in which the labor involved would probably outweigh the result. With the aid of Dr. Jones' reports, we hope to be able to give such specimens as will inspire us with an exalted opinion of the Southern slave-holder.

We begin with the following candid and fearless presentation of the lamentable condition of the negro when the great movement began throughout the South, in which Dr. Jones was not the only, but the most potent factor. It is from his pen, and bears date of 1834:

"The negroes have no regular and efficient ministry; as a matter of course, *no churches; neither is there sufficient room in white churches for their accommodation.* We know of but *five*churches in the slave-holding States built expressly for their use. The galleries or back seats on the lower floor of white churches are generally appropriated to the negroes, when it can be done with convenience to the whites. Where it cannot be done conveniently the negroes who attend must catch the gospel as it escapes by the doors and windows.... From an extensive observation we venture to say, that not a twentieth part of the Negroes throughout the Southern States attend divine worship on the Sabbath.... They have no Bibles to read at their firesides, they have no family altars, and when in affliction, sickness or death, they have no ministers to address to them the consolations of the gospel, nor to bury them with solemn and appropriate services.... For the most part, they depend upon those of their own color, who perform them as well as they know how, if they happen to be at hand."

It must not be inferred from these statements that the neglect was by any means universal; even the sombreness of this picture is relieved by such sunny touches as these: "Sometimes a kind master will perform these offices;" "Here and there a master feels interested for the salvation of his servants, and is attempting something towards it, in assembling them at evening for Scripture reading and prayer, in admitting and inviting qualified persons to preach to them, in establishing a daily or weekly school for the children, and in conducting the labor and discipline of the plantation upon gospel principles. We rejoice that there are such, and that *the number is increasing.*" There were, no doubt, a faithful "seven thousand," if not more, in his, as in Elijah's day.

The reports show a steady improvement in all particulars. We read of churches being built for them, in Liberty county and elsewhere, by slave owners; of men and women stirred up to personal work for the salvation of their people; and of ecclesiastical bodies taking up the matter in good earnest, and resolving and going to work in the neglected field, with the most gratifying results all over the South.

We wish it were in our power to publish the statements *in extenso* proving this, but we can only give specimens culled here and there from the broad and inviting field of these interesting annual reports.

Under the head of individual efforts, take these illustrations: "Detail of a plan for the moral improvement of negroes on plantations, by Thomas S. Clay, of Bryan county, Ga." Mr. Clay was a large rice planter on the Ogeechee river, a bosom friend of Dr. Jones, and living in the adjoining county. In the matter of control upon gospel principles and religious instruction, his large plantation was a model, and his tractate was simply a publication to the Christian world of his mode of thus managing it.

This is said as far back as 1833 of a Virginia planter of Albemarle county, the owner of two hundred and fifty slaves: "He made special efforts to have the gospel preached to them. The consequence was that their whole condition and appearance were improved surprisingly. About thirty became professing Christians, and upwards of ninety joined the temperance society. This gentleman made liberal offers to any minister who would undertake the instruction of his people." This is only one of many examples of planters mentioned as thus faithful and liberal in offering to pay sufficient salaries to any who would preach to their servants.

A gentleman in New Orleans, to whom a report of the Association, and also the report of the Synod of South Carolina and Georgia, had been forwarded, writes as follows: "As the black population of this State are immersed in religious ignorance, the circulation of these reports among the owners of slaves here might, I would hope, awaken them to a sense of their duty." Ordering one hundred and fifty copies of each, he continues: "The system of instruction recommended in the reports had been pursued by me for a long series of years, with signal success to my own private interests, the individual interests and happiness of my servants, and with the result of an entire change in their moral and religious character, and their habits of industry and submission to superiors."

In the report for the year 1843 a lady writes to him: "I have from childhood felt a deep interest, and have been much engaged in the religious instruction of the colored people. I have used Brown's Catechism always. Your book meets fully my views and wishes," etc.

His extensive correspondence all over the South brings to light many a faithful minister with a kindred zeal, giving the half or all his time to the religious instruction of the negro.

In the second annual report he quotes as follows from letters: "A clergymen in Natchez writes: 'I have committed to me the instruction of the negroes on five plantations, in all about three hundred, the owners of whom are professors of religion. I usually preach three times on the Sabbath, and after each sermon I spend a short time catechising. I have occasionally meetings for inquiry.'

"From Oakland College, Mississippi, one writes: 'I have three or four meetings on the Sabbath. I preach once in a fortnight in the church, where about three hundred blacks assemble. Five of the plantations which I attend are within two miles of the church; four others between four and six miles.... I endeavor to visit all the plantations once in two weeks. I go among the people, talk with them face to face, visit the sick, and pray with them.'

"From the Savannah river: "I visit eighteen plantations every two weeks; catechise the children, and pray with the sick in the week. Preach twice or thrice on the Sabbath. The owners have built three good churches at their own expense, all framed, 290 members have been added, and about 400 children are instructed each week.' "

We go outside of our record to add an additional illustrative item, for which we are indebted to the

Southwestern Presbyterian. Speaking of Rev. James Smylie, Rev. Henry McDonald writes in its columns: "In his old age, Mr. Smylie devoted his time exclusively to the religion of the negroes. He had a large congregation of them. In addition to preaching the gospel to them, and reading to them the Scriptures, he taught them the Catechism. He used not only the Primary Catechism, but the Shorter Catechism of the Westminster Assembly. Large classes of them could recite the whole of that catechism. He prepared a catechism for the colored people, which was adopted and recommended by the Synod of Mississippi. This was before Dr Jones published his catechism for them.'

I cannot take up the space necessary to give specimens of the reports, resolutions and narratives passed or adopted by ecclesiastical bodies as they are given at length in these reports. The information which they incidentally communicated shows, that there was a most wonderful awakening upon this subject throughout the Southern Zion. Equal space is impartially given in these reports (which you will search in vain to ascertain the missionary's denominational predilections) to the proceedings of Conferences, Associations, Councils, and Synods; and it is indeed hard to ascertain to which denomination of the one Holy Catholic Church-Methodist, Baptist, Episcopal, or Presbyterian-belongs the honor of marching in the van of this host of southern slave-holding Christians, intent upon conquering by truth and love Africa-in-America for Christ.

The full particulars of this evangelistic work among the negroes by southern Christians may never be written upon earth, but they are certainly inscribed by the recording angel in "The Book of Record of the Chronicles" of Heaven; and to their everlasting honor they will be read out by the King himself in the presence of an assembled universe, what day the "books shall be opened," and "God shall bring every work into judgment, with every secret thing, whether it be good or evil."

CHAPTER XVIII.

THE SEA-BOARD OF SOUTH CAROLINA

"Lands intersected by a narrow frith,
Abhor each other. Mountains interposed,
Make enemies of nations, who had else
Like kindred drops been mingled into one. "

-*Cowper.*

WHILE not foes, only the beautiful and narrow Savannah divides the Georgia sea-board from the South Carolina coast. The same features mark the landscape, the fringe of long, narrow, low islands crowned with live oak, cedar, palmetto and myrtle, and beating back the thundering surf; the wide waving salt marshes, broken here and there by broad, deep estuaries, and everywhere intersected by winding streams, as the tide rises or falls, now filling, now receding from the mud banks, and periodically overflowing, in wide inundation, the meadows; and gleaming like ribbons of silver upon a robe of green, and stocked with fish; high, yellow, sandy, pine-covered bluffs, ornamented with planters' summer residences; broad stretches of rich alluvial lands, waving with golden rice or snowy with Sea Island cotton; boundless forests of long-leaf pine, intersected by swamps; woods fragrant with magnolia and yellow jessamine, and fields and forests abounding with small and large game. Was it a wonder that one of the old navigators (Sir Walter Raleigh, I believe) thus wrote of it: "The great spreading oaks, the infinite store of cedars, the palms and bay trees of so sovereign odor that balm smelleth nothing in comparison; the meadows divided asunder into isles and islets, interlacing one another-these made the place so pleasant that those who are melancholic would be forced to change their humor."

Whether it was due to the sameness of origin, or shaping influence of similar environment, the inhabitants of these two sections of the South, in one of which the writer had his experience of slavery, as before described, were, in many respects, strikingly alike. There was the same refinement and openhanded hospitality, the same fondness in the men for out-door sports, and skillful use of gun and rod, and splendid horsemanship. Their speech, too, was alike. Competent critics have affirmed that nowhere in the world was the English language spoken in greater purity than among the low country people of these two sister States. The relations between slave and master were such as have already been described as prevailing on the Georgia sea-coast The negro population was vastly in excess of the white, but perfectly orderly.

To a friend, a minister of the same church with myself, who, consecrated to the work from student days to the war, labored in this earthly paradise, I am indebted for the following information concerning the efforts of the church to give the gospel to the negro in their region. I give it in his language:

"Let me jot down some statements which may be of use to you:

"1. Previously to the war, the coast of South Carolina was covered by a network of missions among the slaves, conducted by the Methodist Episcopal Church, South. These missions were not the same as the circuits, nor were they embraced in them, but were served by separate ministers devoted to them. They were mainly supported *by the planters*. Besides preaching, the functions of the missionaries included catechising of the children, and visiting the sick on the plantations. It was a great work.

"2. The pastors of the Presbyterian church regularly preached to the colored people, large numbers of whom were members of their churches. In addition to this, some of them preached regularly on plantations, catechising the negro children and youth, and visiting the sick. This was also a great work.

"3. The ministers of other Evangelical denominations partook in similar labors. In the country along the Santee River, Rev. Alexander Glennie, an Episcopal clergyman, devoted special attention to the religious instruction of the negroes." * "Bishop Gadsden, of South Carolina, has this to say of Rev. Stephen Elliott, for so many years the eloquent preacher and revered Bishop of the Episcopal church in Georgia. He built a chapel, at his own expense, for the colored people in Prince William's parish, and resigned his white charge that

* The Rev. Benjamin Webb, a minister of the same church, converted under Dr. Daniel Baker's preaching, did excellent service as a missionary to the blacks in Beaufort District.-*Rev. Dr. B. M. Palmer.*

he might devote his entire care to the population of that parish; doing it 'zealously, faithfully and *gratuitously*.'

"4. In cases in which families, or members of families, were pious, great attention was bestowed upon the instruction of the slaves, especially the children. Sabbath schools on plantations were maintained.

"5. A special enterprise in 1848 was begun for the more thorough-going evangelization of the colored people in Charleston, under the auspices of the Rev. John B. Adger, D. D., and the session of the Second Presbyterian Church. A brick house was built at a cost of seven thousand five hundred dollars. In 1859, in consequence of the enormous growth of the congregation, another church building, which cost twenty-five thousand dollars, *contributed by the citizens of Charleston*, was dedicated. This house was one hundred feet long by eighty broad, and was on a basement, divided into two rooms, which afforded ample conveniences for prayer-meetings, catechising of classes, and personal instruction of candidates for membership. From the first, the great building was filled, the blacks occupying the main floor, and the whites the galleries, which seated two hundred and fifty persons!

"The enterprise began as a branch congregation of the Second Presbyterian church; then became a missionary church, under Rev. J. L. Girardeau, evangelist of Charleston Presbytery; and, finally, in consequence of the admission of white members, a white church with a white session!

"The close of the war found it with exactly five hundred colored members, and nearly one hundred white. Such was its growth from organization as a mission church, in 1857, with only forty-eight members."

Presbyterian readers need not be informed that the faithful minister thus mentioned as connected with this remarkable enterprise is none other than the learned and able Professor of Theology in our beloved school of the prophets, in Columbia, S. C., Rev. John L. Girardeau, D. D.

We doubt if the honored position to which he had been called by the unanimous voice of his church, and for so long a time has ably filled, gives a satisfaction greater than that which fills his soul, when he recalls the work done for his Master among the lowly, gathered within the sacred walls of Zion church, erected by Southern slave-holders for the slave.

We take the liberty of supplementing the brief account already quoted of this remarkable work, by the following fuller statement, which we find in the *Southern Presbyterian Review*, of July, 1854. It is no violence of confidence to say that the article, although anonymous, is from the pen of the honored missionary himself. It is headed, "Report of a Conference by Presbytery (Charleston Presbytery) on the Subject of the Organization, Instruction and Discipline of the Colored People." The debate, covering all the ground as it did, and participated in by men having a practical acquaintance with the subject, must have been deeply interesting, as the report shows it was thorough and able. We extract the paragraph containing evident reference to Zion church, in Charleston:

"The question of the segregation of the blacks from the whites in public worship was not at that time considered, simply because the policy of Presbytery in that matter had already been settled and openly adopted. It has been the almost universal practice of our ministers for many years to convene the people into separate congregations, and dispense to them instruction suited to their exigencies; and at the meeting of this Presbytery at Barnwell, in April, 1847, a formal sanction was afforded to this practice by the extension of its approval and patronage to a scheme, contemplating the establishment of a separate congregation of blacks of the Second Presbyterian church in Charleston.

"The reasons for the collection of the colored people into distinct congregations have been ably stated by Rev. J. B. Adger in a sermon preached in Charleston, May 9th, 1847, and by Rev. Dr. Thornwell, in a critical notice of this discourse, published shortly after its delivery, in the *Southern Presbyterian Review*. The want of room in all our church edifices, the necessity of a style of instruction adapted to the capacities and attainments of the colored population, and their destitute and neglected condition, under the pressure of powerful temptations, constitute cogent arguments in favor of the erection of separate congregations for their benefit. It cannot be denied that there are great advantages resulting from the union of masters and servants in the solemn offices of religion-advantages secured by the conviction produced by this association of a common origin, a common relation to God, and a common interest in the great scheme of redemption through the blood of Christ. But the question, as has been observed, was soon found to be 'partial separation or a partial diffusion of the gospel among the slaves, and an enlarged philanthropy prevailed over sentiment.' It ought to be kept in mind that this separation into distinct congregations does not amount to a compulsory or total exclusion of the servants from access to the churches in which their masters worship. They are at liberty to associate with them in worship whenever they will, while these edifices and religious services, intended especially for their benefit, are standing invitations to those among them for whose welfare no man cares, to participate in the blessings provided by the gospel. It is also to be remembered that a complete separation cannot, and in fact does not, take place under this plan, inasmuch as it contemplates the presence of some white persons-a measure, indeed, made necessary by civil statutes. As, therefore, servants are not debarred from worshiping at pleasure with their masters, as it is expected that in all their assemblages white persons should be present, and as these congregations are served by white ministers, themselves responsible to ecclesiastical courts representing large sections of the community, it is next to impossible that a class worship-as it is frequently objected-should be the result of the enforcement of this scheme, or that it should tend to foster feelings of insubordination and aggravate the prejudices of caste, by connecting them with the institutions of religion."

How far this remarkable and successful experiment of a separate organization in part of colored people, officered entirely by white persons, would, had our civil war not intervened, have won its way into the dense mass of the slave population, and to what extent it would have shaped southern evangelization of the negro, it were idle now to speculate. Besides, its great success in winning from among them scores of precious souls for Christ, the history is important and valuable as furnishing another striking proof of the southern slaveholders' fidelity to the highest interests of the slave.

CHAPTER XIX.
PERSONAL RECOLLECTIONS OF ANOTHER
MISSIONARY TO THE BLACKS.

Rev. Dr. Mallard:

MY DEAR BROTHER,-I hardly know how to communicate personal reminiscences. They would be numerous and detailed. Perhaps I had better not enter the edge of the forest. But I adventure a few which may be of some use to you; if not, throw them out. Of course you do not expect to mention my name.

I remember that before I became a preacher, I used to hold meetings on my father's plantation, the cotton house affording a convenient place of assemblage. Previously, the plantation resounded with the sounds of jollity-the merry strains of the fiddle, the measured beat of the "quaw sticks," and the rhythmical shuffling and patting of the feet in the Ethiopian jig. Now, the fiddle and the quaw sticks were abandoned, and the light, carnal song gave way to psalms and hymns. The congregations were numerous and attentive, and a genuine revival of religion seemed to obtain. I can never forget with what enthusiasm they used to sing their own improvised "spiritual:"

> "My brother, you promised Jesus,
> My brother, you promised Jesus,
> My brother, you promised Jesus,
> To either fight or die.
>
> Oh, I wish I was there,
> To hear my Jesus' orders,
> Oh, I wish I was there, Lord,
> To wear my starry crown."

On another plantation which I was in the habit of visiting, a prayer-meeting was commenced by one or two young men, which became more and more solemn, until the religions interest grew intense, and a powerful revival took place, which involved the white family and their neighbors. The results of that meeting were marked, and some of its fruits remain to this day. If ever I witnessed an out-pouring of the Spirit, I did then.

While teaching school in another place, it was my custom to visit plantations in rotation, on certain afternoons of the week, and catechise and exhort the slaves. I knew of but one planter in that community who objected to this practice, and he was an irrelgious man. On Sabbath, after the regular services of the sanctuary had been held, and the white congregation had dispersed, the negroes would crowd the church building, and, standing on the pulpit steps, I would address them. Their feelings, sometimes, were irrepressible. This was with the sanction of the minister and elders.

While at the Theological Seminary, I only refrained from going on a foreign mission because I felt it to be my duty to preach to the mass of slaves on the sea-board of South Carolina. Having rejected, after licensure, a call to a large and important church which had very few negroes connected with it, I accepted an invitation to preach temporarily to a small church which was surrounded by a dense body of slaves. The scenes on Sabbath were affecting. The negroes came in crowds from two parishes. Often have I seen (a scene, I reckon, not often witnessed) groups of them "double quicking" in the roads, in order to reach the church in time. Trotting to church! The white service (as many negroes as could attending) being over, the slaves would pour in and throng the seats vacated by their masters-yes, crowd the building up to the pulpit. I have seen them rock to and fro under the influence of their feelings, like a wood in a storm. What singing! What hearty hand-shakings after the service! I have had my finger joints stripped of the scarf skin in consequence of them. Upon leaving the church, after the last mournful service with them, and going to my vehicle, which was some hundred yards distant, a poor little native African woman followed me, weeping and crying out: "O, massa, you goin' to leave us? O, massa, for Jesus' sake, don't leave us!" I had made an engagement with another church, or the poor little African's plea might have prevailed. When next I visited that people, I asked after my little African friend. "She crossed over, sir," was the answer. May we meet "when parting will be no more, the song to Jesus never cease!"

The church to which I next went was in a different part of the sea-board of South Carolina. In connection with it, I was ordained, and here my work began in earnest. The congregation included some of the most cultivated gentlemen of the state. They were cordially in favor of the religious instruction of the slaves. The work among them consisted of preaching to them on Sabbath noons, in the church building in which their masters had just worshiped, preaching to them again in the afternoons on the plantations, and preaching at night, to mixed congregations of whites and blacks. This in summer. In winter, I preached at night on the plantations, often reaching home after midnight. Many a time I have seen the slaves gathered on their masters' piazzas for worship, and when it was very cold, in their dining-rooms and their sitting-rooms. The family and the servants would worship together. This was common, and the fact deserves to be signalized. In order better to compass the work, I selected four points in the congregational territory the diameter of which was about twenty miles in one direction, and purposed to secure the erection of meeting-houses which would each be central to several plantations, in order to economize labor and bring the gospel more frequently in contact with the people, by preaching once a month, on Sabbaths, at those points. This plan was prevented of accomplishment by my removal to the missionary work in Charleston. It is curious that after the war the colored people erected houses of worship at those very points.

My last service with the negroes at this church I will never forget. The final words had been spoken to the white congregation, and they had retired. When a tempest of emotion was shaking me behind the desk, the tramp of a great multitude was heard as the negroes poured into the building, and occupied all available space up to the little old wine-glass shaped pulpit. When approaching the conclusion of the sermon, I turned to the unconverted, asked what I should say to *them*, and called on them to come to Jesus. At this moment the great mass of the congregation simultaneously broke down, dropped their heads to their knees, and uttered a wail which seemed to prelude the judgment. Poor people! they had deeply appreciated the preaching of the gospel to them.

Into the details of the work in Charleston I cannot enter. They would occupy too much space. It lasted (with me) from 1854 to 1862. I have sometimes thought I devoted too much time to it. I was absorbed in it. But the labor was not in vain, I trust. Besides Sabbath preaching, most of the nights in the week were spent at the church in the discharge of various duties-holding prayer-meetings, catechising classes, administering discipline, settling difficulties and performing marriage ceremonies. Often have I sat for over an hour in a cold room, instructing individual inquirers and candidates for membership; often have I risen in the night to visit the sick and dying and administer baptism to ill children. I made it a duty to attend all their funerals and conduct them.

Just two extreme instances of dying experience I will give you. One was that of a servant of a distinguished judge. He was dying. As I entered his room, he rubbed his hands together and chuckled with a hilarious delight, like that of a boy going home on Christmas Eve, and exclaimed: "I'm going home! Oh, how glad I am!" So he passed away. Another was that of my own servant. He was reared by me; was a bad boy; when he grew up, attended my church, professed conversion, and was seized not very long after with galloping consumption. He was in terror. His sins filled him with dismay. I

labored with him, but he refused to be comforted. At last, not long before his departure, the light of God's reconciled countenance broke upon the midnight of his soul. From that time he had perfect peace, and breathed his last, I firmly believe, on the bosom of his Saviour. Freely did my tears flow while I was uttering the last words of prayer and exhortation over his encoffined body. His mother, also my servant, died after him, during the war, when I was absent in Virginia. She kept calling for me till she expired. Tell me that there was no true, deep affection of masters to slaves, and slaves to masters! It was often like that between near relatives.

The most glorious work of grace I ever felt or witnessed was one which occurred in 1858, in connection with this missionary work in Charleston. It began with a remarkable exhibition of the Spirit's supernatural power. For eight weeks, night after night, save Saturday nights, I preached to dense and deeply-moved congregations. The result I have given in the general statement prefixed.

The work steadily and rapidly grew, until it was arrested by the war. I could give you some incidents that would be interesting, but time will not permit. One I mention, in which the ludicrous and pathetic were blended, and the saying was fulfilled, that the fountains of laughter and tears are near to each other. After a session had been formed, there came before it for admission into the church a small native African, whose name was Cudjo. The following colloquy occurred between the minister and the candidate: "Cudjo, you want to join the church?" "Yessy, masse." "Cudjo, you love Jesus?" "Yessy, masse; me lub Jesus." 'Cudjo, you expect to see Jesus?" "Oh, yessy, masse; me spec I's see Jesus." "When he sees you coming, what do you think Jesus will say?" "He say, "Cudjo, you come?' I say, 'Yessy, ma'am, I come.' "

Here he struck his hands together, and the session laughed and cried at the same time.

The conduct of this church after the war justified the wisdom of those who projected it. They clung to the white people. One of the first invitations in writing which I received upon my return from imprisonment at Johnson's Island, and while yet in the interior of the State, where my family were refugees, in July, 1865, to resume labor, was from this colored membership, entreating me to come back and preach to them as of old. For years they declined to separate themselves from the Southern Presbyterian Church, and even after its Assembly had, in 1874, recommended an organic separation of the whites and blacks, they continued to maintain an independent position. Only at a late date did they resolve to connect themselves with the Northern Presbyterian Church. But I must close, lest I tire you.

I am, dear brother, yours in the Lord, * * *

I make no apology for giving the above letter just as it was written, in response to my request for personal reminiscences of work among the blacks. It was as not in my heart to alter a word or suppress a line of that which I have not been able to read a single time without tears.

CHAPTER XX.

THE FIRST SOUTHERN GENERAL ASSEMBLY.

'FIRST DAY.

"AUGUSTA, GA., *Dec.* 4, 1861.

"The First General Assembly of the Presbyterian Church in the Confederate States met on this day, at 11 o'clock, in the First Presbyterian Church."

SUCH is the opening sentence of the minutes of that memorable body, in which our distinctive existence as a church began, as reported in the *Augusta Chronicle and Sentinel;* for the use of which I am indebted to the courtesy of Rev. Dr. J. H. Bryson, of Huntsville, Ala.

It was an epoch pregnant with important events in church and state. We pause to rapidly sketch them. South Carolina, seceding from the Union, had been swiftly followed, and in the order here named, by Mississippi, Florida, Alabama, Georgia, and Louisiana. These seven States, meeting by chosen representatives in Montgomery, Ala., had formed a provisional government for one year, to become thereafter permanent and upon the model of that from which they had withdrawn. In April the guns of Fort Sumter opened the fight. Lincoln had then thrown down the gauge of battle in his call for 75,000 men; the Confederate Government had accepted it, in its summons for volunteers. Four more States, halting before, now wheeled into line-Virginia, Arkansas, North Carolina, and Tennessee-eleven in all.

With a daring hopefulness, the capital was now transferred to Richmond, Va.-In the first serious trial of strength at Manassas, the Confederate arms had triumphed; other and less important engagements had marked the first year of the war, the most notable being Price's success at Oak Hill. In his summing up of the year, Alexander

Stephens, in his School History, says: "The contest upon the whole, thus far, was greatly to the advantage of the Confederates, in view of the number of victories achieved and prisoners captured." The enemy had, however, effected a lodgment upon the Atlantic coast of the young Confederacy, by the reduction of the forts at Hatteras Inlet, N. C., and Port Royal, S. C. Fired by accident, the heart of Charleston was then being burnt out by a great conflagration.

In the midst of these exciting events, with the capital threatened by a powerful Northern army, a beautiful Southern city on fire, the white tents of the foe dotting the shores of an adjoining State, and war ships, like watch dogs, guarding all the coast, the delegates appointed by the Southern Presbyteries met to form a Southern General Assembly. In the judgment of most of the commissioners, the separation of the States into two republics, rendered desirable, if not compulsory, two separate churches. But there were other and more imperious causes. The celebrated "Spring resolutions" had made it impossible for a Southerner to be at once loyal to his government and his church. Rev. William Baker, a Southerner, present at the Northern General Assembly the previous spring, in Philadelphia, had accounted for the scantiness of the delegation from the South by the poverty of its ministers. It is certain that some refused to attend because of the danger, and others because they saw that separation of state involved separation of church.

A convention of delegates had previously met in Atlanta, Ga, and invited the Presbyteries at their then approaching fall meetings to appoint commissioners to meet in Augusta, Ga, to form a General Assembly. Meeting at the time appointed, Rev. Dr. John N. Waddel, who, in conjunction with Rev. Dr. John H. Gray and Professor Joseph Jones, of Augusta, Ga., had been selected by a majority of the Presbyteries "to act as a committee of commissioners," nominated Rev. Dr. Francis McFarland as temporary presiding officer. Elected by acclamation, by his nomination Rev. Dr. B. M. Palmer was unanimously selected to preach the opening sermon, and at the next session was elected Moderator by acclamation.

Present as a visitor in attendance upon Rev. Dr. Charles Colcock Jones, then an invalid, but a commissioner from the Presbytery of Georgia, I was an eye-witness of what I now proceed with pleasure to describe and relate.

The place of the first General Assembly was well chosen. Augusta, sitting a queen upon the winding Savannah, on the line between two great commonwealths, and central to the entire Confederacy, was, by its location, its proverbial culture and hospitality, and its handsome First church embowered in its shady grove-a fitting birthplace for the new Presbyterian church.

The personnel of the Assembly was remarkable. The Presbyteries, realizing the gravity of the situation, had sent their oldest, wisest, most experienced, and, in a word, most suitable men. Without attempting to exhaust the list, let me call over some of the names upon its roll, of its men illustrious in divinity and law. The Synod of Alabama sent such men as Rev. Alexander McCorkle, R. B. White, D. D.; Elder Hon. W. B. Webb. Arkansas-Rev. Thos. R. Welsh and the venerable missionary, C. Kingsbury, D. D. From the Synod of Baltimore came John H. Bocock, D. D., Wm. E. Foote, D. D., and Hon. J. D. Armstrong. Georgia sent N. A. Pratt, D. D., John S. Wilson, D. D., C. C. Jones, D. D., Joseph R. Wilson, D. D., and Elders David Ardis, Hon. Wm. A. Forward and Wm. L. Mitchell. Memphis-John N. Waddel, D. D., and Hon. J. T. Swayne. Mississippi-John Hunter, D. D., B. M. Palmer, D. D., James A. Lyon, D. D., Rev. R. McInnis, and Elders Wm. C. Black and David Hadden. Nashville-R. B. McMullen, D. D. North Carolina-R.

H. Morrison, D. D., R. Hett Chapman, D. D., Drury Lacy, D. D., and Elders Prof. Charles Phillips and Hon. J. G.

Sheperd. South Carolina-James H. Thornwell, D. D., Aaron W. Leland, D. D., J. Leighton Wilson, D. D., John B. Adger, D. D., D. McNeill Turner, and Elders Hon. W. Perronneau Finley, J. S. Thompson, Hon. Thomas C. Perrin and Chancellor Job Johnstone. Synod of Texas-R. W. Bailey, D. D., and Rev. R. F. Bunting. Synod of Virginia-Theodorick Pryor, D. D., Francis McFarland, D. D, James B. Ramsay, D. D., Samuel R. Houston, Peyton Harrison, Professor John L. Campbell, Hon. W. F. C. Gregory, etc.

Although to an uncommon extent composed of men entitled by their ability, years, experience and prominence in church and state to lead, there was an entire absence of a domineering spirit, and the utmost freedom of debate, in which there was a general participation. Even that prince of men, of scholars and theologians, Rev. Dr. Thornwell, with all his acknowledged leadership, did not always carry his point, and shaped the actions of the Assembly by the masterly ability with which he advocated his views of the topics discussed, rather than by his powerful personal influence. Never were ecclesiastical debates abler, as might have been anticipated from the material composing this General Assembly. Sitting in the midst of a war of tremendous proportions, with their homes threatened by invasion, and sons, relatives and friends exposed to the deadly hazard of battle, these servants of God spent eleven days in deliberately discussing the problems presented by the times for adjustment, and in perfecting the organization of the infant church. By their wise counsels, that church was provided with all the requisite machinery of executive committees; committees, in accordance with the views of Dr. Thornwell, so long and ably advocated by him, in direct relationship to the General Assembly, taking the place of cumbrous, irresponsible boards. To an executive committee, located in New Orleans, the Indian mission, the only part of the foreign field to which the blockade permitted access, was transferred without a jar; and provision made for the transmission of funds to such southern missionaries outside the United States as wished to retain their connection with our church.

What was determined with regard to the *negro race,*which occupied a large part of the time and attention of this General Assembly, is reserved for the next letter.

Thus our beloved church sprang into existence, like Minerva from Jupiter's brain, full statured and in complete panoply; or, rather, came into being, and by the same creative word as the first Adam did, not a feeble infant, but a strong and grown-up man

Characterized throughout by a prayerful spirit, which seemed, together with the felt gravity of the times, to have repressed every exciting allusion to political and national affairs, this remarkable Assembly, having finished its appointed task, the Moderator announced that there was no further business before it; whereupon, a member, Dr. McMullen, arose and said: "Brethren, the Lord has blessed us in an extraordinary degree. The unanimity and cordiality with which everything has been transacted seems to me to be very remarkable, and it would be to me very gratifying if we could spend an hour this evening in devotional exercises; it would be a delightful closing of this Assembly."

The venerable Dr. Leland, thereupon, slowly rising to his feet, observed: "It becomes us to adopt that proposition and to meet at seven o'clock. Let us this night acknowledge the good hand of God upon us. I do not feel as if we could separate by any sudden adjournment. The best feeling of every heart of this Assembly will be greatly cheered by such a mode of terminating our deliberations. Let us close these meetings with feelings of love and kindness."

Dr. McFarland immediately responded: "That would, indeed, be very pleasant to me. I do trust that we may part with feelings of love and gratitude to Almighty God, such as we never felt before, and that the Moderator (Dr. Palmer), may carry our hearts as one heart up to the heavenly throne.

Said Dr. Pryor: "I think the suggestion of Dr. McMullen eminently proper, and I rise for the purpose of seconding his motion."

The motion adopted, the Assembly coming together in the evening, after the transaction of some matters of business occupying only a few minutes, closed its deliberations by one entire session devoted to worship with the congregation. The 508th hymn was sung, prayer offered by Dr. McFarland, Romans viii. was read, the 580th hymn sung, when the Moderator, Rev. Dr. Palmer, rose and said:

"My brethren, the fulness of this Assembly, drawn from all parts of our extended Confederacy, during a season of extraordinary peril and darkness, is sufficient proof that all our hearts were impressed with the importance of this convention. The discussions through which we have passed, during the session of this Assembly, have opened the fundamental principles of our government, and, to some extent, of our faith. And that we have been able to set this church forward fully equipped, and in doing so to uncover all these principles, and to do it without a jar, is a sufficient proof that we have enjoyed the guidance of God's Spirit. The fact, too, that we have been led to open our hearts towards our brethren of the great Presbyterian family who are not gathered under the same roof with ourselves, opening in the near future the prospect of reunion with those of like faith with ourselves, is an additional proof that our hearts have been moved by the Spirit of grace. And now we are to part; and as we extend the hand of parting there will scarcely be an eye that will not moisten, scarcely a heart that will not throb; we are made to feel, as we return to our several homes, that it has been indeed a privilege to come up here as to a mount of ordinances. Our language will be the language of Peter to his Master on the mount: 'Lord, it is good for us to be here.' "

To this Dr. Pryor responded: "I rise, Moderator, to move that this Assembly be now dissolved. We part to meet no more in this world, but it is pleasant to feel that there is a land where we shall meet again-

'There, on a green and flowery mount,
Our happy souls shall meet,
And with transporting joy recount
The labors of our feet.' "

The 342d hymn was then sung, and with prayer and benediction by the Moderator, the memorable first Southern General Assembly was dissolved, and another like it appointed to meet in Memphis the first Thursday in May, 1862.

CHAPTER XXI.

THE FIRST GENERAL ASSEMBLY AND THE NEGRO; ITS MANIFESTO ON THE SUBJECT TO THE CHURCH UNIVERSAL.

WHATEVER may have been the causes of secession and our civil war, it must be admitted that African slavery was the occasion of both. Although it would not be correct to say that the one side fought for the destruction and the other for the preservation of this peculiar institution, its abolition or continuance was, as the event showed, wrapped up in the issues of the war. The first General Assembly was composed of men who, whether of Northern or Southern birth, were almost, without exception, slaveholders, sincerely convinced of the scripturalness of slavery.

It was with no uncertainty as to their position that this grave and learned and pious assembly of ministers and elders approached the question of the more thorough evangelization of their negro slaves.

Lighted up by the lurid flames of a civil war, the question seemed to have taken on a new interest and assumed larger proportions. With one accord the Assembly seemed to have felt that, in the perilous circumstances surrounding the institution as well as themselves, and the conspicuousness thus given to the Southern Church before the world, there was a special providential call for renewed and intelligent efforts for the salvation of that people, who had now grown in thirty years from two to four millions!

Passing by the incidental references, I shall confine myself to its deliberate utterances upon the whole subject, as they were given in the address to all the churches of Jesus Christ throughout the world, prepared by Dr. Thornwell, and in Dr. C. C. Jones' discourse to the Assembly itself upon the evangelization of the negro.

On the morning of the second day of the session, the following resolution was introduced by Dr. Thornwell, and adopted:

"*Resolved,*That a committee, consisting of one minister and one ruling elder from each of the Synods belonging to this Assembly, be appointed to prepare an address to all the churches of Jesus Christ throughout the earth, setting forth the cause of our separation from the Church in the United States, *our attitude in relation to slavery,* and a general view of the policy which, as a church, we propose to follow." (Italics mine.)

That committee, appointed by Dr. Palmer, the Moderator, in the same session, contained the following distinguished names: James H. Thornwell, D. D., Theodoric Pryor, D. D., F. K. Nash, C. C. Jones, D. D., R. B. White, D. D., W. D. Moore, J. H. Gillespie, J. L. Boozer, R. W. Bailey, D. D., J. D. Armstrong, C. Phillips, Joseph A. Brooks, W. P. Finley, Samuel McCorkle, W. P. Webb, William C. Black, T. L. Dunlap, and E. W. Wright.

On the eighth day their report, taken up from the docket, was, without debate or a dissenting voice, adopted as the utterance of the Southern Church, and under the following resolutions

"*Resolved,* That the Address to the Churches of Jesus Christ throughout the world, reported and read by Rev. Dr. Thornwell, chairman of the special committee appointed for that purpose, be received, and is hereby adopted by this Assembly.

"*Resolved,* That three thousand copies of this address be printed, under the direction of the Stated Clerk, for the use of the Assembly.

"*Resolved,* That the original address be filed in the archives of the Assembly, and that a paper be attached thereto, to be signed by the Moderator and members of this Assembly."

It was a deeply interesting spectacle when, at the calling of the Assembly's roll, each member approached the Clerk's desk and signed his name to this magnificent state paper, which bears the stamp of the acute intellect and broad genius of the chairman, Dr. Thornwell. We can afford space for only a few extracts from this historical document, and only upon the attitude of the Southern Church toward slavery:

"And here we may venture to lay before the Christian world our views as a church upon the subject of slavery.

"In the first place, we would have it distinctly understood that, in our ecclesiastical capacity, we are neither the friends nor the foes of slavery; that is to say, we have no commission either to propagate or abolish it. The policy of its existence or non-existence is a question which belongs exclusively to the state. We have no right to enjoin it as a duty, or to condemn it as a sin. Our business is with the duties which spring from the relation; the duties of the master on the one hand, and of their slaves on the other. These duties we are to proclaim and to enforce with spiritual sanctions. The social, civil, political problems connected with this great subject transcend our sphere, as God has not entrusted to his church the organization of society, the construction of governments, nor the allotment of individuals to their various stations. The church has as much right to preach to the monarchies of Europe and the despotisms of Asia the doctrines of republican equality, as to preach to the government of the South the extirpation of slavery. The position is impregnable, unless it can be proved that slavery is a sin. Upon every other hypothesis it is so clearly a question of state, that the proposition would never for a moment have been doubted had there not been a foregone conclusion in relation to its moral character.

"Is slavery a sin?

"In answering this question as a church, let it be distinctly borne in mind that the only rule of judgment is the written Word of God. The church knows nothing of the intuitions of reason, or the deductions of philosophy, except those reproduced in the sacred canon. She has a positive constitution in the Holy Scriptures, and has no right to utter a syllable upon any subject, except as the Lord puts words in her mouth. She is founded, in other words, upon express *revelation*. Her creed is an authoritative testimony of God, and not a speculation, and what she proclaims she must proclaim with the infallible certainty of faith, and not with the hesitating assent of an opinion. The question, then, is brought within a narrow compass. Do the Scriptures, directly or indirectly, condemn slavery as a sin? If they do not, the dispute is ended, for the church, without forfeiting her character, dares not go beyond them. If men had drawn their conclusions on this subject only from the Bible, it would no more have entered into any human head to denounce slavery as a sin, than to denounce monarchy, or aristocracy, or poverty. The truth is, men have listened to what they falsely consider as primitive intuitions, or as necessary deductions from primitive cognitions, and then have gone to the Bible to confirm the crotchets of their vain philosophy. They have gone there determined to find a particular result, and the consequence is that they leave with having made, instead of having interpreted, Scripture. Slavery is no new thing. It has not only existed for ages in the world, but it has existed under every dispensation of the covenant of grace in the church of God. Indeed, the first organization of the church as a visible society separate and distinct from the unbelieving world, was inaugurated in the family of a slaveholder. Among the very first persons to whom the seal of circumcision was affixed, were the slaves of the father of the faithful, some born in his house and some bought with his money. Slavery again appears under the law. God sanctions it in the first table of the Decalogue, and Moses treats it as an institution to be regulated, not abolished; legitimated, not condemned. We come down to the age of the New Testament, and we find it again in the churches founded by the apostles, under the plenary inspiration of the Holy Ghost. These facts are utterly amazing, if slavery is the enormous sin which its enemies represent it to be. It will not do to say that the Scriptures have treated it only in a general and incidental way, without any clear implication as to its moral character. Moses surely made it the subject of express and positive legislation, and the apostles are equally explicit in inculcating the duties which spring from both sides of the relation. They treat slaves as bound to obey, and inculcate obedience as an office of religion-a thing wholly self contradictory, if the authority over them were unlawful and iniquitous.

"But what puts the subject in a still clearer light, is the manner in which it is sought to extort from the Scriptures a contrary testimony. The notion of an explicit and direct condemnation is given up. The attempt is to show that the genius and spirit of Christianity are opposed to it; that its great cardinal principles of virtue are against it. Much stress is laid upon the Golden Rule, and upon the general denunciations of tyranny and oppression. To all this we reply, that no principle is clearer than that a case positively excepted cannot be included under a general rule. Let us concede for a moment that the laws of love and the condemnation of tyranny and oppression seem logically to involve, as a result, the condemnation of slavery; yet if slavery is afterwards expressly mentioned and treated as a lawful relation, it obviously follows, unless Scripture is to be interpreted as inconsistent with itself, that slavery is by necessary implication excepted. To say that the prohibition of tyranny and oppression include slavery, is to beg the whole question. Tyranny and oppression involve either the unjust usurpation of, or the unlawful exercise of, power. It is the unlawfulness in its principle or measure, which constitutes the core of the sin. Slavery, therefore, must be proved to be unlawful, before it can be referred to any such category. The master, indeed, may abuse his power, but he oppresses not simply as a master, but as a wicked master.

"But apart from all this, the law of love is simply the inculcation of universal equity. It implies nothing as to the existence of various ranks and gradations in society. The interpretation which makes it repudiate slavery would make it equally repudiate all social, civil and political inequalities. Its meaning is, not that we should conform ourselves to the arbitrary expectations of others, but that we should render unto them precisely the same measure which, if we were in their circumstance, it would be reasonable and just in us to demand at their hands. It condemns slavery, therefore, only upon the supposition that slavery is a sinful relation; that is, he who extracts the prohibition of slavery from the Golden Rule begs the very point in dispute.

"We cannot pursue the argument in detail, but we have said enough, we think, to vindicate the position of the Southern Church."

I add to the argument one single sentence more from this splendid vindication of the position of our Southern Presbyterian Church: "We feel that the souls of our slaves are a solemn trust, and we shall strive to present them faultless and complete before the presence of God."

Here I must, *per force,* stop in my quotations from this able paper, in which one knows not which most to admire, the logic or the rhetoric, the reasoning or the piety. Let it now be recalled that the entire Assembly affixed their signatures publicly to this document; as well, the venerable Dr. A. W. Leland, of northern birth; "a southerner," as he well expressed it once in a time of great excitement in South

Carolina, "a southerner not of necessity as one born in that section, but by choice," and Rev. Dr. James H. Thornwell, a southron by descent, birth, and in every fibre of his being. Some would say, Why write of a dead issue? To this we make answer: Truth never dies, for it has the years of God, the immortality of its Author. What was scriptural and therefore right before the war, is both still. God has in his providence abolished African slavery, because he saw fit, and because his Word always taught, as the southerner believed, that, other things being equal, "to be free is better." But Divine Providence is not in conflict with the Divine Word. Tried by the Bible, slavery was not sin, nor southern slaveholders sinners because of it. And there is something inspiring in that conviction of right which enabled these hundred or more ministers and elders to stand immovable in the tossing billows of that dreadful conflict which was occasioned by, and resulted (with the regrets of none) in the abolition of American slavery in America.

CHAPTER XXII.

THE FIRST GENERAL ASSEMBLY AND THE NEGRO-THE ADDRESS OF DR. JONES ON THE RELIGIOUS INSTRUCTION OF NEGROES.

THE last appearance, I believe, of the "Apostle to the Blacks,"as, in a former letter, Rev. Dr. Charles Colcock Jones was styled, in any ecclesiastical body, was before that convened in Augusta, Ga., in 1861. "Perhaps I shall not be with you, brethren, next year," he had said, in excusing himself from the chairmanship of an important committee, appointed to report to the next Assembly. He never went to another, until he was summoned by the angel of death to "the general assembly of the firstborn, which are written in Heaven."

Appointed chairman of the Committee of Domestic Missions, he used this language on the subject ever near to his heart: "That the great field of missionary operations among the colored population falls more particularly under the care of the Committee of Domestic Missions; and that committee be urged to give it serious and earnest attention, and the Presbyteries to co-operate with it in securing pastors and missionaries for the field."

This last suggestion was made the special order for discussion on the evening of December 10th; and Dr. Jones invited to address the Assembly upon the subject. We state, in passing, that in the debate which followed, it was resolved that a pastoral letter be prepared upon the subject, to be reported for action to the next General Assembly, the chairmanship of which Dr. Jones, on the plea of ill-health, as before stated, declined. His Address the Assembly directed to be published. I have in my bound volume of pamphlets a copy of it. It has not lost its power to stir my soul, although committed for a quarter century to the cold custody of the printed page; its effect at the time of its delivery was marvelous. Let an eye-witness describe the occasion and the address.

The large audience-room of the beautiful church was filled from pulpit to door by commissioners and people. The speaker, as he walked up the aisle, by the feebleness of his gait, and somewhat bowed form, created the impression of age which was not confirmed by his short-cropped light hair, with scarcely a silver thread, and his noble, intellectual, spiritual and benevolent face, without a seam or wrinkle. Unable, from weakness, produced by a wasting palsy, to stand, he took the position in our Lord's day assigned the teacher. Sitting, but with free use of arms and hands, in impressive gesture, he held the immense audience spellbound, in almost absolute stillness, for an hour and a half, while he plead for the souls of the poor slaves, to whose salvation his noble life, now rapidly, as he and we well knew, drawing to its close, had been consecrated. Back of the speaker there was what the old rhetoricians laid down as an essential of true oratory-character. The audience saw before them one, of whom a fellow-commissioner, Rev. Dr. B. M. Palmer, has recently used this language, in the obituary of his only daughter: "Her distinguished father, it need not be told, by his intellectual strength and culture, and still more by the majesty of his character, acquired the highest distinction which could be conferred in the church which he served.

He was twice called to the chair of history and polity in the Theological Seminary at Columbia, S. C., and then to discharge the important function of Secretary of Home Missions in the Presbyterian Church, long before the separation caused by the late civil war. Yet all these public honors were voluntarily surrendered by this man of God, that, without fee or reward, he might become a missionary to the slaves in his native county. By this act of self-abnegation, he endeared himself to the people of God throughout the land, and won a distinction to himself beyond that of princes or titles to confer."

Beginning with the thought that the meeting in the interests of Domestic Missions was but a continuation of that held the previous evening in behalf of Foreign Missions, since the field was one and the work the same, he rapidly sketches the territory occupied by the Confederate States, its physical features, productions and population. He then skilfully introduces the subject of the negro; his peculiar relation to the whites, relative numbers of the two races, and sketches the history of his introduction into the United States. Noting the fact with approval that the Confederate Congress had passed an act prohibiting the slave-trade, and that for a long period the increase of the negro had not been by importation, but by birth, he remarks that "the natural increase of the negroes under a genial climate and mild treatment has kept pace with that of the whites, but not exceeded it, and that increase will continue, although for good reasons (white emigration?) the white population will make the disparity of numbers between the two classes greater and greater at every census." He then, in feeling and eloquent language, emphasizes the value of the slave as a fellow immortal, dwells upon his close relation to the master, his importance to society as a producer of values, and draws from all these considerations powerful arguments for his evangelization. He then, with all his moving oratory, urges to their help a church which had, as he affirmed, only "partially fulfilled" her duty to this people, in the providence of God, now thrown exclusively upon the southern people for the gospel, and closes with practical suggestions as to the best methods of performing this her acknowledged duty.

No analysis can do justice to the address, and we shall append to our imperfect summary, as samples of its moving oratory, a few extracts.

Paying the race a deserved compliment for its good behavior throughout its history in this country, he asks:

"*Whence* came this people? Originally from the kraals and jungles, the cities and villages, of the torrid regions of Africa, wonderfully adapted by constitution and complexion to live and thrive in similar latitudes in all the world. They are inhabiters of one common earth with us; they are one of the varieties of our race-a variety produced by the power and in the inscrutable wisdom of God; but when, and how, and where, lies back of all the traditions and records of men. These sons of Ham are black in the first hieroglyphics; they are black in the first pages of history, and continue black. They share our physical nature, and are bone of our bone and flesh of our flesh; they share our intellectual and spiritual nature; each body of them covers an immortal soul God our Father loves, for whom Christ our Saviour died, and unto whom everlasting happiness or misery shall be meted in the final day. They are not the cattle upon a thousand hills, nor the fowls upon the mountains, brute beasts, goods and chattels, to be taken, worn out and destroyed in our use; but they are men, created in the image of God, to be acknowledged and cared for spiritually by us, as we acknowledge and care for the other varieties of the race, our own Caucasian or the Indian, or the Mongol. Shall we reach the Bread of Life over their heads to far-distant nations, and leave them to die eternal deaths before our eyes?

"*What is their social connection with us?*They are not foreigners, but our nearest neighbors; they are not hired servants, but servants belonging to us in law and gospel; born in our house and bought with our money; not people whom we seldom see and whom we seldom hear, but people who are never out of the sight of our eyes and hearing of our ears. They are our constant and inseparable associates; whither we go they go; where we dwell they dwell; where we die and are buried, there they die and are buried; and, more than all, our God is their God. What parts men most closely connected in this life from each other, that can only part us from them, namely, crime, debt, or death. Indeed, they are with us from the cradle to the grave. Many of us are nursed at their generous breasts, and all carried in their arms. They help to make us walk, they help to make us talk, they help to teach us to distinguish the first things we see and the first things we hear. They mingle in all our infantile and boyish sports. They are in our chambers and in our parlors, and serve us at every call. We say to this man 'Go,' and he goeth; and to another 'Come,' and he cometh; and to another 'Do this,' and he doeth it; they are with us in the house and in the field; they are with us when we travel on the land and on the sea; and when we are called to face dangers, or pestilence, or war, still are they with us; they patiently nurse us and ours in long nights and days of illness; our fortunes are their fortunes; and our joys their joys; and our sorrows are their sorrows; and among the last forms that our failing eyes do see, and among the last sounds our ears do hear, are their forms and their weepings, mingled with those of our dearest ones, as they bend over us in our last struggles, dying, passing away into the valley of the shadows of death! My brethren, are these people nothing to us? Have we no gratitude, no friendship, no kind feelings for all that they have done for us and for ours? Have we no heart to feel, no hand to help, no smiles to give, no tears to shed on their behalf?

No wish in our inmost soul that they may know what we prize above all price, our precious Saviour, and go with us to glory, too?

"*What is their value as an integral part of our population, to ourselves, to our country, and to the world itself?*To ourselves, they are the source, in large measure, of our living, and comprise our wealth, in Scripture, our 'money.' Our boatmen are they on the waters; our mechanics and artisans to build our houses, to work in many trades; our agriculturists to subdue our forests, to sow and cultivate and reap our lands; without whom no team is started, no plow is run, no spade, nor hoe, nor axe, is driven; they prepare our food, and wait upon our tables and our persons, and keep the house, and watch for the master's coming. They labor for us in summer's sun and in winter's cold; to the fruit of their labor we owe our education, our food and clothing, and our dwellings, and a thousand comforts of life that crowd our happy homes; and through the fruit of their labors we are enabled to support the gospel and enjoy the priceless means of grace. Brethren, what could we do without this people? How live and support our families? And have they no claims upon us? Are they nothing more than creatures of profit and pleasure? Are the advantages and blessings of that close connection between us in the household to be all on one side? Has our Master in heaven so ordained it? I will reverse the question of the apostle to the Corinthians and put it in the mouth of your servants, and make them ask it of you, their masters: 'If we have sown unto you carnal things, is it a great thing if we shall reap your spiritual things?' "

This is what he beautifully says to pastors, in urging them not to forget this part of their charge:

"Give notice to the master on what evening you will be with him, and that you will preach or lecture for his family and household. Right gladly will he welcome you; the family and plantation will be all astir-"our minister is coming to preach to us this evening.' Tea is over, the time for the meeting is at hand. The little children beg to sit up to meeting; one servant takes the books and lights, another the chairs and stand. Everything is nicely arranged, and you are directly in presence of bright faces, and your psalm is sung with spirit and power, your prayer and your sermon fall on many attentive ears, and the hearty thanks of your humble parishioners fill you with gladness. At the close, you will speak an encouraging word to the members of the church, and shake hands with the aged, and perhaps step in to see some sick and afflicted one. You will also enquire how well the children and youth attend the plantation Sunday-school; and if you do not impart joy to the household, and go away a happier Christian and a more blest minister, we shall bid farewell to years of experience and observation in this field of labor."

Insisting on a high order of qualification in the missionary to the blacks, and thorough preparation for his pulpit labors, he says this of his pastoral duties:

"And as a good shepherd he will follow them into the highways and hedges, into their own plantations and into their own sick chambers, and speak unto and pray with them. He will perform their marriage ceremonies and attend their funerals, and follow them to their graves, and go in and out before them, with the Bible in his hands, in the fear of the Lord. He will become a star in the right hand of the Saviour before them, and they will rejoice in his light, and learn to sing his hymns. and quote his precepts, and authority, and argue by his knowledge, and take him to be their friend, and seek his instruction in times of difficulty, and his comfort in their times of sorrow, and bring their families to him for instruction and for his blessing; and when they die, they will wish him to preach their funeral sermon. He will be happy with the people, and they will be happy with him; as much so as weak and sinful and partially sanctified ministers and people can be in this world. Whenever he meets them he speaks kind words, and receives kind words in return. He is not ashamed of them, and they are glad in him; and when he rides along the road, and they are at work in the field, he flings over the fence amongst them, a cheerful 'Good morning! good morning to you all!' In a moment, every eye is up, and they catch his voice and person, and return his salutation with a hearty good will, with rapid inquiries after his welfare, and their loud and happy conversation dies on his ear as he leaves them behind!"

A more tender and poetic and yet eloquent paragraph it would be hard to find in any address, than that which I now close an account of an address, which stirred my soul to its depths, as it did others, and sent me (a lover of the race from childhood, and since manhood a worker among them) to my home and charge, determined (the best proof of the speaker's power) to work for their salvation as I had never done before.

Imagine the effect of hearing this man of God, manifestly drawing near to the grave, unable even to stand, give this as his experience and parting word to his ministerial brethren, whose face they were to see in our highest court no more!

"Yes, my brethren, there is a blessing in the work! How often, returning home after preaching on the Sabbath day, through crowds of worshippers, sometimes singing as they went down to their homes again, or, returning from plantation meetings, held in humble abodes, late in the starlight night, or in the soft moonlight silvering over the forest on the roadside, wet with heavy dews, with scarcely a sound to break the silence, alone, but not lonely; how often has there flowed up in the soul a deep, peaceful joy, that God enabled me to preach the gospel to the poor?

"And now that this earthly tabernacle trembles to its fall, and these failing limbs can no more bear me about, nor this tongue, as it was wont, preach the glad tidings of salvation, I look back, and varied recollections crowd my mind, and my eyes grow dim with tears, I pray for gratitude for innumerable mercies past, for forgiveness for the chief of sinners, and for the most unfaithful of ministers, for meek submission for the present, and for an assured hope in a precious Saviour for the future. Oh, my brethren! work while the day lasts, 'for the night cometh when no man can work;' for the shadows of that night, even while the day lasts, may fall upon you and stop you in your way, ere its deep darkness shut you around in the cold grave, no more to be removed until the Son of Man shall come in his glory, to the judgment of the great day."

CHAPTER XXIII.
CONDUCT OF THE NEGRO DURING THE WAR.

THE celebrated Emancipation Proclamation was clearly a war measure, whose sole purpose was the crippling of the enemy. It went into operation imperfectly during the war within the Federal lines, and became effectual only at its close. Indeed, it is said that some Indian slaveholders in the Everglades of Florida have only recently found out that their negroes are free. The conduct, therefore, of the negro before emancipation includes his conduct during the war.

The facts which I am about to relate are notorious, and have passed into history, but it will be useful to recall them. What I shall relate is the result largely of my own observation, and of what I have learned from the lips of actors in the scenes described.

It will be convenient to divide the subject; and I

will first speak of the conduct of the negro in vast regions of the South never invaded by a Federal army

Here let me promise that there was no discernible difference in the conduct of the negroes as the war progressed and the area of the doomed Confederacy constantly narrowed, and the news percolated the country that the object of the approaching armies was their liberation. Whether it was due to the habits of industry and subordination engendered by two centuries of American slavery, or to the intrinsic inoffensiveness of the race, it is certain that their conduct under most trying circumstances was above all praise, and constitutes a debt which Southerners should be neither reluctant to acknowledge nor slow to pay.

As a rule, there was no insubordination among them, although the master's eye and hand were absent, much less threat of, or execution of violence. With the entire arms-bearing male population-"conscription robbing (as it was said) the cradle and the grave"-withdrawn, they, under their negro drivers and occasional overseers, and mainly under the direction of mistresses, advised by letter from time to time by masters at the front, tilled the fields, harvested and sold the crops, and protected the defenseless families of men fighting against their freedom! Absolutely, women and children felt and were safer then than they are now in some parts of the South.

Let me now refer to their conduct within the Federal lines. Some bad slaves, and a few, mostly young and foolish negroes, fascinated by the large promises of freedom which, in their ignorance, they mistook for exemption from work and governmental support, followed in the wake of the liberating armies, until their privations forced them home again. The sufferings of these poor creatures made the name given to them by the Federals, "contrabands," a synonymn of wretchedness.

The great mass of them within the changing army lines remained quietly in their homes, and took care, with a beautiful fidelity, of the families of their owners. In not a few instances, their treatment by the Federals was not calculated to awaken any ardent admiration of their deliverers. In Liberty county, for example, they robbed servant and master with perfect impartiality, not only carrying off the clothing of the absent master and present servant, but exchanging their infested underclothing for that of the negro women!

The conduct of the negro in Liberty county, Ga., during what is still called "Sherman's Raid," is doubtless a fair specimen of their conduct elsewhere under similar circumstances. As such I give now the testimony of two eye witnesses; and first quote from a brief journal of the experience of the only daughter, now deceased, of Rev. Charles Colcock Jones, D. D., on her father's plantation home, "Montevideo," Liberty county, Ga.

When Sherman, in his unopposed march from Atlanta to the sea, struck the fortifications around Savannah, which occasioned only a short halt, his great army flattened out all over the adjoining country and lived upon its rich resources. Our guard said they had a perfect picnic in our county. For a month or more, three lone females and five little children were exposed to the constant visits of foraging parties of his troops. I quote from the journal written upon one of my old blank books, in part occupied with memoranda of texts to be fashioned into sermons:

Tuesday, Dec. 1, 1861,-Mother rode to Arcadia this morning, thinking the Yankees were no nearer than Way's Station (in an adjoining county), and lingered about the place until late in the afternoon, when she started to return to "Montevideo," and was quietly knitting in the carriage fearing no evil: Jack was driving. Just opposite the Girardeau place, a Yankee sprang from the woods and brought his carbine to bear upon Jack, ordering him to halt, then lowered it so that he could bring it to bear either upon the carriage or Jack, and demanded of mother what she had in the carriage. She replied: "Nothing but my family effects." "What have you in that box behind your carriage?" "My servant's clothing" "Where are you going?" "To my home." "Where is your home?" "Nearer the coast." "How far is the coast?" "About ten miles. I am a defenceless woman, a widow; have you done with me, sir. Drive on, Jack." Bringing his gun to bear on Jack, he called out: "Halt!" He then asked, "Have you seen any rebels?" "We have a Post at No. 3." He then said: "I would not like to disturb a lady, and if you take my advice you will turn immediately back, for the men are just ahead, and they will take your horses and search your carriage." Mother replied: "I thank you for that," and ordered Jack to turn. Jack saw a number of men ahead, and mother would doubtless have been in their midst had she proceeded. (Pursuing, under great difficulties, a circuitous route, for the Confederates had taken up the bridges, and with a faithful negro acting as her voluntary scout, she reached her home and anxious daughter at nine o'clock at night. The journal continues:)

I was truly rejoiced to hear the sound of the carriage wheels, for I had been several hours in the greatest suspense, not knowing how mother would hear of the presence of the enemy. (Learning, meanwhile, of the presence of Federal soldiers in the neighborhood, she continues:) Fearing a raiding party might come up immediately, I had some trunks of clothing and other things carried into the woods, and the carts and horses taken away, and prepared to spend the night alone, as I had no idea mother could reach home. After ten o'clock Mr. M-came in to see us, having come from No. 3, where a portion of Hood's command was stationed. Mr. M-staid with us until two o'clock, and fearing to remain longer left, to join the soldiers at 4 1/2, Johnson's Station. He had exchanged his horse for C-'s mule, as he was going on picket duty and would need a swifter animal. This distressed us very much, and I told him I feared he would be captured. It was hard to part under this apprehension, and he lingered with us as long as possible, and prayed with us just before leaving.

Wednesday, Dec. 14.-Mother and I rose early, thankful no enemy had come near us during the night. We passed the day in great anxiety. Late in the afternoon, Charles (the servant man) came into the parlor, just from Walthourville, and burst into tears. I asked what was the matter. "Oh!" he said, "very bad news. Massa is captured by the Yankees, and says I must tell you to keep a good heart." This was a dreadful blow to us and to the poor little children; M-especially realized it and cried all evening!...

Thursday, Dec. 15.-About ten o'clock mother walked out upon the lawn, leaving me in the dining-room. In a few moments Elsey came running in to say the Yankees are coming, I went to the front door and saw three dismounting at the stable, where they found mother. I debated whether to go to her or remain in the house; the question was soon settled, for in a moment a stalwart Kentucky Irishman stood before me, having come through the pantry door. I scarcely knew what to do. His salutation was: "Have you any whiskey in the house?" I replied: "None that I know of" "You ought to know," he said in a very rough voice. I replied: "This is not my house, so I don't know what is in it." Said he: "I mean to search this house for arms; but I will not hurt you." He then commenced shaking and pushing the sliding doors and calling for the key. Said I: "If you will turn the handle and slide the door you will find it open." The following interrogation took place: "What's in that box?" "Books." "What's in that room?" "You can search for yourself." "What's in that press?" "I do not know, because this is mother's house, and I have recently come here." "What's in that box?" "Books and pictures.""What's that, and where is the key? " "My sewing-machine; I'll get the key." He then opened the side door, and discovered the door leading into the old parlor." "I want to get into that room" "If you will come around I will get the key for you." We passed through the parlor; he ran up the stairs and commenced searching my bed-room. "Where have you hid your arms?" "There are none in the house, you can search for yourself." He ordered me to get the keys to all my trunks and drawers. I did so, and he put his hand into everything, even a little trunk containing needle-work, boxes of hair, and other small things of this description. All this was under color of searching for arms and ammunition! He called loudly for all the keys; I told him my mother would soon be in the house and she would get the keys for him. While searching my drawers he turned to me and asked. "Where is your watch?"

I told him: "My husband has worn it, and he was captured the day before at Walthourville." Shaking his fist at me he said: "Don't you lie to me; you have got a watch." I felt he could have struck me to the floor, but looking steadily at him, I replied: "I have a watch and chain, and my husband has them with him." "Well, were they taken when he was captured?" "I do not know, for I was not present." Just at that time I heard another coming up the stairsteps, and saw a young Tennessean going into mother's room, where he commenced a search. Mother came in soon after and got her keys, and there we were following two men around the house, handing them the keys and seeing almost everything opened. The Tennessean found a box, and hearing something rattling in it, he thought there must be coin within it, and would have broken it open, but Dick prevented him. Mother got the key, and his longing eyes beheld a bunch of keys. In looking through the drawers to mother's surprise, Dick pulled out a sword which belonged to her brother, and had been in her possession for thirty years, and she had forgotten it was there. Finding it to be so rusty that they could scarcely draw it from the scabbard, they concluded it would not kill many men in the war, and did not take it away.

He turned to mother and said: "Old lady, haven't you got some whiskey?" Mother said: "I don't know that I have." "Well," said he, "I don't know who ought to know if you don't." (The ladies were afraid of the results of their getting liquor.) Mother asked him "if he would like to see his mother and wife treated in this way, her house searched and invaded?" "Oh!" said he, "none of us have wives." Whilst mother walked from the stable with one from Kentucky, he had a great deal to say about the South bringing on the war. Mother asked him, "if he would like to see his mother and sisters treated as they were treating us." "No!" said he, "I would not, and I never do enter houses, and shall not enter yours;" and he remained without, while the other two men searched. They took none of the horses or mules; all being too old.

A little before dinner we were again alarmed by the presence of five Yankees, four of them dressed as marines. One came into the house; a very mild sort of a man. We told him the house had already been searched. He asked "if the soldiers had torn up anything!" One of the marines came into the pantry and asked if they could get something to eat. Mother told them they were welcome to what she had prepared for her own dinner, and if they chose they could eat it where it was. So they went into the kitchen, and cursing the servants, ordered milk, potatoes, and other things. They called for knives, etc. Having no forks out but plated ones, mother sent them, but they ordered Milton to take them back, and tell his mistress to put them away in a safe place, as a parcel of d-d Yankees would soon be along, and they would take every one from her. We hoped they would not intrude upon the dwelling, but as soon as they finished, the four marines came in, and one commenced a thorough search, calling for all the keys. He found difficulty in fitting the keys, and I told him that I would show them to him, if he would give me the bunch. He said he would give them to me when he was ready to leave the house. He went into the attic and instituted a thorough search. Taking a canister, containing some private papers belonging to my dear father, he tried to open it. Mother could not find the key immediately, and told him he had better break it; but she could assure him it contained nothing but papers. "D-n it," he said, "if you don't get the key, I will break it; I don't care." In looking through the trunks, he found a silver goblet, but did not take it. One of the marines came in with a Secession rosette, which mother had given Jack to burn. We were quite amused to see him come in with it pinned upon his coat. He had taken it from Jack. This one was quite inclined to argue about the origin of the struggle. After spending a long time in the search, they went off, taking one mule; they left the carriage horses, as mother told them they were seventeen years old. In a short time we saw the mule at the gate; they had turned it back. After they left, I found that my writing-desk had been most thoroughly searched, and everything scattered, and all little articles, as jewelry, pencils, etc., abstracted. A gold pen was taken from my work-box. Mother felt so anxious about Kate King (a neighbor and friend) that she sent Charles and Niger to urge her to come to us; but they did not reach South Hampton, as they met a Yankee picket which turned them back, and took Charles with them to assist in carrying horses to Midway, promising to let him return.

Friday, Dec. 16.-Much to our relief, Prophet came over this morning with a note from Kate, to know if we thought she could come to us. Mother wrote her to come immediately, which she did in great fear and trembling, not knowing but that she would meet the enemy on the road. We all felt truly grateful she had been preserved by the way.

About four in the afternoon we heard the clash of arms and noise of horsemen, and by the time mother and I could get down stairs we saw forty or fifty men in the pantry, flying hither and thither, ripping open the safe and crockery cupboards. Mother had some roasted ducks and chickens in the safe. These the men seized, tearing them to pieces like ravenous beasts. They were clamoring for whiskey and for the keys. One came to mother to know where her meal and four were. She got the pantry key, and they took out all that was there, and then threw the sacks across their horses. Mother remonstrated, but their only reply was, "We'll take it." They flew around the house, tearing open boxes. One of them broke open mother's work-box with an andiron. A party of them rifled the pantry, taking away knives, spoons, forks, tin plates, cups, coffee-pot, and everything they wished. They broke open the old liquor case and carried off two of the gallon bottles, and they drank up all the blackberry wine and vinegar which mother had in the case. It was impossible to utter a word, for we were completely paralyzed by the fury of the mob. A number of them went into the attic, into a little store-room mother had there, and carried off twelve bushels of meal which mother had put there. Mother told them they were taking all that she had for herself, daughter, friend, and five little ones, but scarcely any regarded her voice, and those that did laughed and said they would leave a sack, but they only left some rice, which they did not want, and poured a little meal upon the floor. They called for men's shirts and men's clothes. We asked for their officer, hoping to make some appeal to him, but they said "they were all officers." We finally found one man who seemed to have a little show of authority, which was indicated by a whip which he carried. Mother made an appeal to him, and he came up and ordered the men out. They brought a wagon and took another from the place to carry off their plunder. It is impossible to imagine the perfect stampede through the house, all yelling, cursing, quarreling, and going from one room to another in wild confusion. They were of Kilpatrick's Cavalry; and we look back upon their appearance in the house as some horrible nightmare! (In narrating this scene afterwards, the writer of the diary said to me, "The atmosphere seemed blue with oaths.") Before leaving, they ordered all the oxen to be gotten up early next morning.

Saturday, Dec. 17.-About four o'clock we were roused by the sound of horses, and from that until sunrise squads of six and ten were constantly arriving. We felt a dark time of trial was upon us, and we knew not what might befall us. Feeling our weakness and peril, we all went to prayer, and continued in prayer for a long time, imploring personal protection and that the enemy might not be permitted to come nigh our dwelling. We sat in darkness, waiting for the light of morning to reveal their purposes. In the gray twilight we saw one man pacing before the kitchen, and afterwards found that he had voluntarily undertaken to guard the house, as far as he could. In this we felt that our prayer had been answered. As soon as it was light, Kate looked out and discovered an officer near the house, which was a great relief of our feelings. Mother went down and begged him that he would not allow the soldiers to enter the house, as it had already been three times searched. He said "it was contrary to orders for men to be found in houses, and the penalty was death; and, so far as his authority extended, no man should enter the house." He said they had come on a foraging expedition and intended to take provisions, etc. Upon mother inviting him in to see some of the work of the previous evening, he came in and sat awhile in the parlor. The Yankees made the negroes bring up the oxen and carts, and took all the chickens, turkeys, etc., that they could find; they also took off all the syrup from the smoke-house and some fresh pork. Mother saw everything stripped from the premises, without the power of uttering one word. Finally they rolled out the carriage, and took that to carry in it a load of chickens(!). Everything was taken that they possibly could. The soldier who was our voluntary guard was from Ohio, and when mother thanked him and told she wished she could make him some return for his kindness, he said: "I could not receive any, and only wish I were here to guard you always." They took off Jack, Pulaski, June, Martin, little Pulaski, and Ebenezer, also George, but said they might all return if they wished, as they only wanted them to drive their carts as far as their wagon train. One said the carriage should return, and afterwards said mother must send for it if she wanted it. He knew very well that this was impossible, as all the harness had been taken from the place. A little later mother walked to the smoke-house, and found an officer taking her sugar, which had been put to dry; he seemed a little ashamed at having been caught, but did not return the sugar. He was mounted upon Audley King's pet horse, and said as he rode off: "How the man who owns this horse will curse the Yankee who took him when he goes home and finds him gone!" He had Mr. King's servant mounted upon another of his horses, and no doubt knew he was near (in hiding) when he made the remark. Immediately we went to work, removing the salt and the remainder of the sugar into the house, and while we were doing so a Missourian came up and advised us to get everything into the house as quickly as possible, and he would protect us while doing so. He said he had enlisted to fight for the Constitution, but since then the war had been turned into another thing, and he did not approve this Abolitionism, for his wife's people all owned slaves. He told us, what afterward proved false, that ten thou-infantry would soon pass through Riceboro, on their way to Thomasville. Soon after this some twenty rode up, and caught me having a barrel rolled toward the house, but they were very gentlemanly and only a few of them dismounted. They said "the war would soon be over, as they would have Savannah in a few days." I told them "Savannah was not the Confederacy." They replied: "We admire your spunk." They inquired for all the large plantations. All the poultry that could be found was taken off. Squads came all day until dark. The ox-wagons were taken to Carlarotta to be filled with corn.

Sabbath, Dec. 18.-We passed this day with many fears, but no Yankees came to the lot, although many went to Carlarotta (another settlement on the same plantation), and were engaged in carrying off the corn, the key of the corn-house having been taken from Cato (the driver) the day before. A day comparatively free from interruption was very grateful to us, although the constant state of apprehension in which we were, was very distressing. In the afternoon, while engaged in reading and seeking protection from our Heavenly Father, Capt. Winn's Isaiah came, bringing a note from Mr. M-to me, and from Mr. John Stevens to mother, sending my watch. This was the first intelligence from Mr. M-. How welcome to us all, although the note brought no hope of his release, as the charge against him was taking up arms against the United States. Capt. Winn had been captured, but released. We were all in such distress that mother wrote Mr. Stevens, begging him to come to us. We felt so utterly alone, that it would be a comfort to have him with us.

Monday, Dec. 19.-Squads of Yankees came all day, so that the servants scarcely had a moment to do anything for us out of the house; the women finding it entirely unsafe for them to be out at all. The few stray chickens and some sheep were killed. These men were so outrageous at the negro houses, that the negro men were obliged to stay at their houses for the protection of their wives, and in some instance rescued them from the hands of these infamous creatures.

Tuesday, Dec. 20.-A squad of Yankees came after breakfast, rode into the pasture, drove up some oxen, and went into the woods and brought out mother's horse wagon, to which they attached the oxen. Needing a chain for the purpose, they went to the well and took the chain from the buckets. Mother sent out to-.

Here the journal ends. I add, that when the first troops searched the house, the ladies, offering to help them in their examination for cannon and muskets in their trunks(!), adroitly flung the linen taken from those first examined over trunks containing all their silver; and leaving everything just as the first invaders of the home had deranged it, subsequent marauders were misled; and so woman's wit got the better of Yankee shrewdness. Throughout all this long and trying experience, in which three unprotected females and five young children were exposed to the rudeness of Sherman's soldiers, the servants, one and all, old and young, were perfectly respectful and faithful; indeed, our families, ruthlessly robbed of all provisions by United States soldiers, would, for all they cared, have suffered from hunger, had it not been that their slaves provided them with food.

The last entry in the journal was December 20th. January 4th, the writer of the journal (her husband a prisoner in Savannah, with good prospect of being sent for the war to a Northern prison), and with fifty Yankee soldiers clamoring to enter the house, who only were kept out by the pluck of a lone woman, a friend, gave birth to a daughter. The invaders would not be said nay, until this lady said: "You compel me to be plain, and to say that a child is being this moment born in the house;" when they raised a general yell, stuck spurs to their horses, and disappeared down the avenue!

In response to my request to know how the negroes behaved in Liberty county during the raid, the wife of one of our best known Georgia pastors then in charge of the old Midway church, Liberty county, gives this as her experience:

"Tell Cousin R-that the negro population in Liberty county during the war were restrained by their religious training and teaching; and we owe dear Uncle Charlie (Rev. Dr. C. C. Jones) a debt of gratitude. Defenceless women and children, and not the first act of violence or depredation! On the contrary, constant acts of kindness! Our people fed us during the raid, and served us faithfully, until we left the county months afterwards to come up here, and they were all polite and respectful. I told our people, while they were now free to the end of the chapter, I was free, and no longer obliged to take care of them, and they must now take care of me and of themselves, and not to follow the army, but to stay on their own plantations and provide for themselves; that they could see the army could not take care of their own soldiers without tearing down our corn-houses; and as Sherman's army encamped on our place (Lambert plantation), and killed the cattle, sheep, geese, levelled the fences and burnt the cotton-house, and tore down the corn-houses to get at the corn before their eyes, they saw the necessity of caring for themselves. Syphax came and told us of the destruction of the things at Arcadia (furniture and a fine piano); and then these reports from Lambert plantation reminded me of the adverse messengers Job received in ancient times. There were so many false reports of citizens being killed and wounded, and some true, that the bewilderment of a war is a terrible thing. The searching of the houses for fire-arms by the soldiers was terrible. But a better appointed army than the Yankee army the sun never saw, or one more obedient to orders. At a signal the house would be swarming with them, and at a signal they would be out of it as quickly. Mr. B-says Gen. Sherman never was in Liberty county himself. The man who came with twelve others was so convinced by my words of Mr. B-'s innocence, that he released him immediately, charging him to remain in the house, but Mr. B-, saying he was safe in the discharge of his duty, visited his people as usual, going to Montevideo to see dear aunt Mary Jones and all the family. The behavior of the whole colored population was wonderful in the extreme. I doubt if we white people had been placed in the same trying position, we would have behaved as well. The soldiers would tell them: 'Now if you want anything out of that house, go in and take it,' but they did not take the first thing, as far as I know; indeed, they had all they needed, and they had to watch their own clothes and things. Augustus, our carriage driver, told me they had taken his best coat and his watch; and all of Mr. B-'s they could get hold of, they carried off. And they seemed to need fresh garments sadly. Matilda, servant, swept a pair of discarded pants from the piazza, which she said she was afraid to touch!

.... I saw a Yankee soldier take Mr. B-'s watch, after he returned to us from the other side of the Alatamaha. The Yankees never came into our houses at night (they were mortally afraid of bushwhackers), which was a blessing."

I believe I could not have presented more vivid or correct illustrations of the noble conduct of the negro during the war, than that furnished in the above journal and letter of two eye-witnesses, the wives of well-known living Presbyterian ministers.

CHAPTER XXIV.
CONCLUSION.

I HAVE now, through the blessing of God, finished the self-appointed and not unpleasing task assumed many months since. The reader and the writer have traveled, let us hope not without mutual pleasure and profit, over a wide territory. Beginning with the author's reasons for writing, and with a sketch of the topics as they lay in his mind, to which he has in the main adhered, he has given some account of his connection with slavery and slaves, painted from memory the old plantation, recalled the occupation and sports which made it a paradise to children, described the houses, food, clothing, physicking and work of the negro, and his marriage and family relations.

He has next presented the photograph of a curious character; and, with the aid of his own memory and the contributions of two Southern authors, given specimens of the only literature peculiar to the negro slave.

With a loving and loyal hand he has sketched the history of a remarkable church, that of his fathers, and drawn from memory "Sacrament Sunday" in the same, in which master and slave commemorated together the Saviour's dying love. Then he has attempted to sketch in outline the life of one who more than any man deserves to be known as "the Apostle to the negro slave." Then followed a rapid outline of his labors among and for them, a recital of anecdotes preserved by him, illustrative of negro character and religious experience. Then was given rapid sketches of work done in the same field by other ministers, individuals, churches and communities, including the history of a remarkable enterprise in a Southern city, and the personal and tender reminiscences of another beloved missionary to the blacks. The series has been fittingly closed with a sketch from memory of the first General Assembly, and a report of its work for the salvation of the slave, and the testimony of eye-witnesses to the noble conduct of the negro during the war.

Those who, without prepossession or prejudice, have read these letters, must be convinced, if they needed any proof, that African slavery in America was not what some in their ignorance, envy or malice have portrayed it. That, with its confessed evils and occasional abuses, it had many redeeming qualities. No one who credits the statements of the competent and truthful eye-witnesses given, will for a moment doubt that in innumerable instances the bond which bound master and slave had almost the kindness, tenderness and strength of the ties which connect dear kindred. It must also be perfectly clear that, to a large extent, Southern Christians appreciated their responsibility, and endeavored to discharge it toward the souls of a people, in the providence of God, with no agency of theirs, committed to their care; that the slaves were not, as a general rule, regarded as mere chattels, but as immortal beings, for whose religious instruction they (the masters) would be held accountable by their common Master in heaven.

No one that I have met since the war regrets their emancipation; no Christian would again freely assume the responsibility, felt to be so heavy by not few in the olden time. We have no harsh or angry feelings against those who, without compensation, annihilated the larger part of the former wealth of the South, and reduced our people temporarily almost to beggary. Surely we entertain no feelings of resentment toward those who, without being consulted, were suddenly and without any preparation invested with the responsibility and (in their intellectual condition) dangerous privilege of citizenship. Our own beloved church, the Southern Presbyterian, has shown every disposition to help them religiously since the war, as far as they would accept our aid. We feel that their great need as citizens and as immortal beings, is a pious and educated ministry. In accordance with this view, there has been established our seminary, the Tuskaloosa Colored Institute in Alabama. Open to students of all denominations, it is our institute by which we hope to raise up, for their future separate church, an efficient Presbyterian ministry. The work already done by this seminary tells for itself, and it is highly creditable to the ability of its professors. Its graduates are, in their humility, modesty, elocution and ability, an honor to their Alma Mater. One of the graduates, with a white associate, is now in Africa, a missionary of the Southern Presbyterian Church.

One important end of these letters will have been accomplished if they shall have fostered the kindly feeling already binding the two races together, if they have awakened on our part a deeper and more helpful sympathy with them in their infant enterprise, the establishment of an African Presbyterian church in the South, and if they shall have drawn to the aid of our Tuskaloosa Institute the generous pecuniary support of Christians North and South.

And now I close my letters as the Psalmist did his psalms, and with his doxology: "Blessed be the Lord God, the God of Israel, who only doeth wonderful things, and blessed be his glorious name forever, and let the whole earth be filled with his glory. Amen and Amen."

Made in the USA
Monee, IL
06 January 2025

76148698R00085